HER UNRAVELING

A GUIDE TO UNDERSTANDING THE POWER OF YOUR EMOTIONS AND HOW TO ALIGN WITH YOUR INTUITION

CASSIE JEANS

KATY SPIEWAK | BRANDY STRATTON | JENNIFER LEIGH | ROSE FINLAY
JASMINE CABANAW | OLIVIA SHWETZ | ANGELA JOY EBY
JESSICA DE CASTRO | LIZ PRAX | MEGAN HARMONY
KHADOMA COLOMBY | MAGGIE BOWLES | ERIN SAARI | SABRINA GREER

Her Unraveling: A Guide to Understanding the Power of Your Emotions and How to Align with Your Intuition

2020 YGTMama Media Co. Press Trade Paperback Edition.

Published in Canada, for Global Distribution by YGTMama Media Co.

www.ygtmama.com

For more information email: publishing@ygtmama.com

ISBN trade paperback: 978-1-989716-02-1

To order additional copies of this book: publishing@ygtmama.com

Editing by Christine Stock

Cover design by Amber Christine

Interior design & typesetting by Doris Chung

Table of Contents

Author Bios

Preface

Intuition.
Heart's desire.
Filling the void.
Questioning the past?
Curious about the future.
Trying to stay in the present.
Overloaded with information.
Googling to find the answers.
Wondering who we are.
Wondering where we fit.
Dissecting history to gather our brokenness together.
Learning to love the brokenness and harnessing its power.

Intuition.
Emotions.

These two evoke an internal compass that has been guiding women for centuries. It is almost impossible to articulate the depth of these sentiments, and so we choose to share a part of our life story. In sharing our individual experience, this somehow magically brings us together and raises the vibration of harmony. Can this book encompass in totality the vast experiences that women have throughout the world? Absolutely not. But perhaps it has the ability to spark conversations, to continue the journey of speaking from one's experience, and to bridge the gaps that are still present in our ever-changing world.

Cynthia Occelli writes:

> *"For a seed to achieve its greatest expression, it must come completely undone. The shell cracks, its insides come out and everything changes. To someone who doesn't understand growth, it would look like complete destruction."*[1]

Her Unraveling reflects the reality of what this great expression requires of us. It would seem each author represented in this book has learned the art of living a grateful life, she has encompassed her art of surrender amid the trials and tribulations of life, and in no way has this been a perfect experience. It's been messy, raw, tumultuous. Silver linings have shown up, God has lifted heavy hearts at times, the Universe has called, the spirit within each woman has reminded her of her own wild and divine nature, and many times, nature has restored her soul.

And so we get a glimpse into the many facets of a life experience. We get a snapshot of what it means to rise up even when it feels like we are being dragged down. We get to read a piece of someone's story and somehow it allows us to accept our own. To love our own experience.

To learn from those who went through their own shadows and found the light within their very soul.

Wise women are rising up all over the world. This book is a small representation of the sheer diversity that makes our world beautiful. The sharing of story matters. This is how we have passed down knowledge, this has been how we learn to navigate different experiences, this is how we remember our humanity.

Emotions

We chose to focus on emotions because they are a big part of our human experience. We have learned a variety of things about emotions over the years, and in some ways, emotions have been viewed as a weakness. This book attempts to empower emotions instead of suffocating them. Emotions provide a compass for us to know where we thrive in our life, our relationships, our work, our families. Negating emotions is quite costly to our health. Stress is an emotion that is often overlooked by living the "busy" lifestyle. Sadness is rarely allowed space to be felt, and sometimes we are taught to numb this emotion with a variety of tactics from scrolling social media to chemical addictions. Loneliness has been called an epidemic in some countries and so we think if we have a social life worth Instagramming about somehow that means we won't experience loneliness. Pain is taught to be avoided. Depression is scripted drugs. The goal is to be happy, happy, all the time, and this drive to be happy can create the opposite emotion, thus creating the shame of thinking that somehow life will never measure up to what we think it's supposed to be.

I think we are realizing on a grand scale how intricate every organism is on the planet. We are realizing that one way does not work for us, and as we tune out the noise and tune into our hearts, we find this incredible sanctuary of light within ourselves. We start facing our shadows instead of running from them; we start understanding emotions as sacred instead of lumping them into two categories: good or bad. All are sacred. All guide us to live a more whole life. And this is beautiful all in itself. The results of learning the art of listening to our emotions are peace, joy, gratitude, love, understanding, compassion, surrender, forgiveness. Listening to our emotions creates a different energy within the body, the mind, the heart, and the soul. By honoring emotions, we honor our life, and in exchange, we start to live more wholly.

Intuition

The great foundation of a wild woman's soul. Intuition. The resounding voice within. The gentle whisper. The uneasiness in the stomach. The alarm bell. The sweat, the pricks in the pits. The roar that cannot be silenced. All within. How beautiful is that? The thing we can barely find words for but we know it's there. Like an aura of light, like a song that reminds us of God, like a secret communication between us and nature. Our intuition is alive within us. It's the breath between sentences and often the call to come home to what we innately know. It is a process of learning how to listen to our intuition. When we were children it was there as a steady companion, but for many of us, we stopped paying attention to it as we got older. There were other desires, other experiences, other aches we had to journey that would eventually guide us back to our inner balance and sanctuary. Intuiton, again, does not mean perfection. It means a heightened ability to decipher the bullshit and act accordingly. It allows us to stop compromising our soul for the sake of a faulty relationship. It allows us to stop appeasing others' opinions at the cost of our free voices. It allows us to call it quits when things have been broken beyond repair. It allows us to question without needing the answer and to honor the sacredness of our life. It is a steady compass and shows up in many ways to guide and protect us. In Clarissa Pinkola Estes' book called *Women Who Run with the Wolves,* there is an abundance of wisdom about a woman's intuition, and after reading this book, I recommend following up with Estes'. *Women Who Run with the Wolves* inspired me personally to create *Her Unraveling* and to welcome other writers to be a part of the process. Collective voices joining together to share some incredibly powerful life experiences heighten a woman's intuition as well. She is finally seen. She feels understood. She is no longer silenced. She is able to heal. She desires to let the wounds become a scar of strength. She breathes deeply and can finally let go. She finds herself and quite likes what she sees.

That is a prayer for all women who read this book and all who are on their journey of healing. That through it all she will feel good in her soul, in her body, in her heart, in her mind. That she would have the courage to break away from what doesn't bring her joy and stand up for her life. Your intuition will know when it's time to set your heart free.

Chapter 1

Finding Inner Peace Through Unrest

Dr. Katy Spiewak, D.C.

With a perpetual smile, Dr. Katy Spiewak lives her life from a place of integrity, kindness, and truth. She has been a chiropractor for over ten years, serving both humans and a variety of animals, both large and small. Born, raised, and currently living with her young family in a small town in Ontario, Katy finds happiness in the simple pleasures of life. A self-proclaimed homebody, her happiest place is in the kitchen creating and preparing healthy, nutritious meals. She also enjoys staying active, connecting with friends, and being with her family. On the other side, she has a strong zest for travel and exploring all the wonders of the world. Her passion has always been helping others, and she has a keen gift for finding a positive spin on life. Being honest about the challenges of motherhood and sharing her journey, her goal is to connect, nurture, and support other mothers on their path. Katy is always excited to learn more, expand herself further, and be her best while motivating others to feel alive and live their truth along the way.

Dr. Katy Spiewak, D.C.

www.themommamoment.com

the_momma_moment

The Momma Moment

"When I feel completely me, I am living in the moment with the contentment of peace and happiness in my heart and soul."

At ten years into my chiropractic practice and ample amounts of perseverance, hard work, and passion, I had created a thriving business. On the outside, I had ticked off every major goal I thought I desired in life. I had arrived at the place I dreamed of: an awesome career, a loving and supportive husband, and two beautiful, healthy children. I was happy—or as happy as I thought I could be. I have always thrived on a life of busyness. From a young age, I was continuously tackling my never-ending "to-do" list, and I loved the satisfaction of checking off those boxes. Perfectionism stemmed from a childhood where I was the "good child" and the "easy one." I come from a loving family who have the best of intentions for me, but I can recall from a very young age a feeling of not wanting to be a burden to my parents or anyone else. I spent a good portion of my youth retracted like a turtle in its shell. I rarely took a misstep growing up, which created a habit of perfectionism and emotional silence. This structure left me with a deep burden of emotional confinement within, which felt like a restriction and contraction of my soul. I felt suffocated like a prisoner in my own body. I held onto these ideals comfortably until my first son came along.

For me, the greatest gift of self-discovery has been becoming a mother. I love my children with all my heart, but in full disclosure, their arrival in my life has been a turbulent ride. Everything that I had carefully constructed in my life and in my mind quickly and fiercely unraveled with the birth of my son. The demands and multitasking of motherhood sent me into a whole new vortex of trying to maintain a sense of control. On the inside, I felt like I was drowning most days. I was living in a fairly constant state of stress trying to balance everything that life required of me.

I can remember one particularly bad day when I was practically functioning on zero sleep, had changed a third blow-out diaper, was returning emails and phone calls for work and tackling endless laundry, and was trying to maintain my life in the way that I expected of myself while trying to soothe a cranky baby. I looked deep into my teary eyes in the mirror and said to myself out loud, "Why did I do this to my life?" It was not a proud moment as a mother. Looking back on that time still makes my heart sink. I felt overwhelmed, exhausted, and joyless. My cup was dry, and I had very little to give to anyone. It just felt like a whole lot of work with little enjoyment. The demands of my business, life, and motherhood left me constantly reacting to each situation with little downtime. If I wasn't focused on something that needed to get done, I was worried about something that had already happened. There was no "living in the moment" for me. I yearned for calm, simplicity, and presence. In the big picture I had nothing to complain about, but the daily grind felt chaotic and exhausting. I tried so hard to be "well." I did all the healthy things that are supposed to make you feel good. There were certainly fleeting moments of contentment, but they never lasted very long. It felt like I was always waiting to get through the next thing to find enjoyment and stillness, but then something else would come along that needed to get done. I can see now that I was burning out fast.

The tipping point came when two close family members, who I had admired and adored my whole life, came face-to-face with cancer. It was a major wake-up call for me. I could no longer go on living that way. I needed to find a way to be more present and enjoy this beautiful life that I was lucky enough to be gifted. I decided then to make some changes. First, I started simplifying my practice and my thoughts. I found a way to compartmentalize work away from family and my personal time. I put up healthy boundaries and learned to be okay with saying a confident "no." For the first time in my life, I started putting my needs ahead of others. As tough as it was to get to this point, it felt absolutely freeing to take control of my time. Clearing and simplifying my mind and thoughts turned out to be the most challenging component for me. I had always believed I was a naturally positive person, but when I really began to critically assess my thoughts, I was all over the place. I realized that I tended to focus and dwell on feelings that made me feel anxious. Trying always to be perfect meant I was pretty hard on myself. I found it very difficult to stay present, sit in the moment, and simply be without having my mind spin restlessly.

There always seemed to be something to plan or worry about. I had dabbled in meditation through my practice of yoga for many years, but it felt intimidating and beyond my capabilities to pursue on my own. Still, I started a very irregular meditation practice of sitting in quiet solitude and focusing on breathing. Recognizing those unsupportive thoughts, watching them go by and choosing to release them brought me immense peace and relaxation. Even with my limited knowledge, meditation brought more contentment and happiness to my daily life.

I began to feel the space between my thoughts and understand true presence. I believe that things, opportunities, and people enter your life at the right time, and this was certainly true for my introduction to daily meditation.

An acquaintance, who has since become one of my closest friends, happened to bring up in conversation a meditation course that they were enrolled in. I was so surprised and intrigued that this topic would come up at this specific time in my life. I had been searching for more information but wasn't quite sure how to go about finding it. It seemed to arrive at the perfect moment. They encouraged me to take the course. All at once, I found so much peace and freedom with learning to meditate. Where I once felt overwhelmed, assuming that meditation was "above" me, it soon became a natural start to my day, a nonnegotiable daily routine. Since beginning this practice, there has not been a day that goes by that I don't make space for meditation. It has become as important to me as getting dressed and brushing my teeth every morning. I think of it as my mental shower. It is the piece of my puzzle that was missing as it has helped me realize that my true happiness is completely within myself. It feels so effortless, beautiful, and powerful. Meditation has not only amplified my kind and loving nature, but it has also given me the ability to release judgments toward myself and others, live with intention, express my true self, find clarity, and love freely. It provides me with a more present deeper connection to the people around me so that I can give them the best version of myself.

There are so many different ways to practice meditation. For me, meditation is not about "not thinking." We continuously breathe, our hearts always beat, our fingernails grow, and our minds are always active. I am not a Buddhist monk who has committed to a life of meditation. I am a busy mom, wife, and businesswoman. I believe that in our harried culture, taking time daily to tune out the external world and listen to the messages from your heart and soul is critical for optimal well-being. The daily grind can leave us feeling depleted, joyless, tired, and unable to give to others, but when we tap into the awareness of our own truth, we can express openness, vulnerability, intention, connection, and fully serve our purpose. We are naturally hardwired for negativity. It is our basic "fight or flight" mechanism, and our brains trick us into thinking that is what is needed for survival. As mothers (especially new mothers), we live having to constantly respond to our children's needs. This requirement forces us to stay in a fairly constant sympathetic/"fight or flight" state of our nervous system, which creates a tremendous amount of stress and strain on our bodies (physically, mentally, and emotionally). Meditation helps to bring us into a restful and restorative parasympathetic state. Getting to know this feeling versus the former has been very helpful to me in knowing when I need to take a break and change my situation. When life is throwing me too much external "noise," I always have meditation to reconnect me with space, clarity, and presence. It takes work and determination to shift the way we think. I no longer let any negative thoughts invade my space. Certainly they are around me and I think about them, but I never allow those unsupportive thoughts to stay. Every day is an opportunity to learn, grow, and make the best decisions for me. Each session in meditation is a unique experience depending on what is happening in my life. Some days are simply easier than others. It is absolutely normal to feel all types of emotions, no matter their label; however, I have learned to choose thoughts that are positive and release the ones that don't serve my true self. I may not be quite as "on the ball" as I used to be, but to my surprise, I still get everything accomplished in a more present, peaceful, and content way.

It sounds so silly now, but I used to stress about things like running low on peanut butter or having a full hamper of dirty laundry. When I am reminded of these little things in everyday life that once used to make me feel so anxious and realize that they barely phase me anymore, I feel free. We are bombarded with different stimuli all day long through many avenues: work, social media, family, driving our vehicles, and even going to the grocery store. Challenging situations arise wherever we go, but we have the choice to choose our thoughts. We have the choice to decide how we evaluate, process, and react to situations, and how we internalize them. Choosing kindness, love, and compassion, even in those difficult moments, gives me complete freedom. Finding harmony and balance is a daily task. For me, it is especially true with raising children.

I like to refer to motherhood as "consciousness bootcamp!" My boys challenge me many times a day to choose my feelings. I used to rarely feel a sense of ease where I could let my guard down with my children. I rarely felt present or could actively engage in playfulness with them. Being able to maintain a steady calm even when my sons fight or my toddler purposefully dumps a bowl of soup on the floor, has a tantrum in the grocery store checkout, or scribbles on our newly painted walls keeps me grounded. There are certainly still frustrating, teeth-clenching moments, and I don't always act like the "ideal mom," but when I can crack a smile, have a little chuckle, and remind myself that they are learning and embrace the moment, I know that I am where I am supposed to be. I lead with an open heart in situations, and it has created a beautiful flow and ease to my every day.

What I have come to understand about myself is that there are two fundamental things I long to feel in each and every present moment. Where I am content is when I feel both peace and happiness in the core of who I am. I believe that underneath all our wants and desires is a simple feeling of peace and happiness. This experience is unique and individual.

For me, it is having optimal health, safety, family, friends, presence, and freedom (to name a few). To others, it can mean something completely different. I have allowed myself to surrender to peace and happiness and trust that life will guide me in the right direction if I keep this feeling in my heart and soul. That means trusting the decisions that I make and allowing life to unfold as it is meant to, even if it is not the plan that I have in my mind. I am still an "achiever," but I have relinquished control from doing it perfectly and it is incredibly freeing. It also has allowed me to truly appreciate each and everyone's individuality.

I believe the uniqueness of each person should be celebrated, and my desire for all other beings in this world is for them to find their own peace and happiness no matter how they choose to arrive there. I now smile more, I have more energy, and I forgive completely; my thoughts are simpler, I walk taller, I exercise harder, and I have better focus. I feel more love for others, I am kinder, more compassionate and patient with my children, I enjoy moments in full presence, and I see more beauty in the complexity of our amazing world. In return, I have been able to accept and truly appreciate all the amazing and sometimes surprising gifts (both big and small) that have come my way. As the late Dr. Wayne Dyer said, "Change the way you look at things and the things you look at change."[1] For all those things and so much more, I am truly grateful for meditation. It has helped shape my life in a new direction, one where I am free to express my true self with ease, grace, and harmony. Not a day goes by that I don't meditate. It's really not worth missing all the benefits that it brings me. If my story resonates with you at all, I recommend giving meditation a try. It has truly changed my life, and I hope it will do the same for you.

~ I am incredibly lucky to have amazing parents who supported my passions and helped me in any way that they possibly could to make my dreams a reality. Your many gifts and sacrifices will always be cherished. Thank you to the many teachers along the way who taught me a deep appreciation of science and nature and instilled a love of lifelong learning. To the ones I didn't realize were teachers at the time, I am grateful. My life is abundantly full of beautiful friends and family. Thank you for believing in me and loving me. To my husband, Todd: You are my everything. I love having you beside me on this crazy journey of life. Lastly, to my sons, Ryder and Rowan: You challenge me every day to show up as the best version of myself. You are my biggest inspirations and greatest teachers. Thank you.

Dr. Katy Spiewak, D.C.

Chapter 2

Presence Is a Gift

Brandy Stratton

Brandy Stratton is the radiant essence behind "Presence Is a Gift." She has been a beacon of warmth while wearing a smile through considerable life challenges. Her journey into emotional depth began when she lost her mother to cancer at the age of twelve. This submersion was the radical rewriting of Brandy's innermost understanding of what life could hold. Brandy is a grateful mother of five-year-old twins, who has taken life's moments in stride. Brandy never considers any moment to be a failure, only a groove to develop her intuition, which includes being a two-time college dropout and divorcee. Brandy is a Reiki Master Teacher who pursues deep connection with others on their journey of healing and is eminently dedicated to sharing her luminosity. She is a tenacious believer of seeking guidance from within and trusting your truth with practice in presence.

Brandy Stratton

@benevolentbrightheart

benevolentbrightheart

"I wanted to feel everything, the pain, the comfort, the unknown."

At the age of twelve, I lost my mom to cancer. To my brother and me, she was our world, and I felt I lost my only friend. I didn't really know who I was, but I am certain she did. My mom was a person who radiated pure love. You knew how she felt about you because her love created a cord from her heart to yours, and everyone felt the same way about her. I had always been a happy person. Part of that happiness came from being loved by this beautiful person I had called mom. Living with my dad and stepmother happened within a week or so of her death, and that's when the feeling of being entirely alone and lost set in. The experience taught me to go inward, to watch my thoughts, but I had no clue how to get out. I spent the following ten years living in my mind, shy and scared, but always with a smile on my face. Unknowingly, the safe walls I built around me from fear of experiencing that loss kept me from finding my truth and following my intuition.

I have come to realize that my smile is a direct connection to my spirit, my true essence, and through the years has acted as my shield, my cushion, and my source. Although the external light in my life was extinguished when my mom passed, and the darkness had a grip on my heart, I survived. It was my spirit that lit me up, guiding me as if unaware; however, intuitively I knew that I would be okay. It kept me aligned with my divine purpose and held me during the unraveling and desperate need to understand life.

How is it that life can feel on track and full of purpose and then suddenly feel empty? My large extended family had helped me bandage my wound, but my feelings about life and how it works and what it means were questions lingering, born of my unfledged heart.

I went on to get married when I was twenty-seven to a man who I thought was my soul mate. He was the first person to see me. He supported my growth and was my personal cheerleader in moments of difficulty. I tried to support him, but at the same time, it drained me. A constant drip of my energy went toward his mental health challenges. I learned how to be a caregiver, especially during the year my mom had endured her illness, and it continued into my marriage.

Over the years, my sweet existence became troubled. Life for me had carried on but felt like it had flatlined. No excitement, just the same day on repeat. I began to feel anxious every day, and the feeling of being lost crept back in. There were layers of confusion that I was drowning in, and the more I tried to keep going, the deeper I went. I needed change. I needed help, and my search for someone or something that could pull me out of these heavy spaces was the only thing on my mind. I began taking private yoga classes with a therapist, and I quit my overwhelming job and found one with less responsibility and more fun. Yet, I needed more. This is when I found out I was having twins! Oh my.

It was not a surprise for me as I had sensed it deep in my gut, literally. Pun intended! What if they tell us we are having twins? This experience was my first realization of how in tune I was with my intuition. It was as if I had an internal guidance system that worked like a map, I trusted it, and the more I connected to my heart, the more information it unlocked. I previously believed in chance or coincidence. No longer was this the case. I knew I was having a boy and a girl. I left it a surprise until birth for everyone else. It felt amazing to believe something to be true and it be so. Within me was a beautiful connection to self, and it was an amazing experience to watch as it unfolded. I was falling in love with myself for the first time in my life at thirty-two years old. Feeling everything and anything, I felt aligned with my purpose of being a mother.

Pregnancy was a breeze up until the end of my third trimester when I was diagnosed with preeclampsia. That's when the doubt and feelings of inadequacy built up and I could sense difficulties ahead. With my then-husband unable to give me the support I needed, I was alone and lost. Again. My relationship with my extended family had drifted, I had no close friends, so I went within and tried to build a wall of protection. My strength grew inside, and my experiences had taught me how to push through. Without a doubt, it was going to be hard. There would be times that I thought I couldn't survive another day. Nevertheless, I would. I was determined to be happy and that everything would be as it should be.

My twins' birth did not go as I had hoped. The candles and birthing pool remained a dream. The decision for a cesarean section was made for me, and from there I felt my personal power slip away. Although my feelings of helplessness were palpable, I would come to understand that my life was and is full of experiences that are meant to be shared. The sensations I felt after surgery were overwhelming, warning me that something wasn't right. I looked at my then-husband and made a comment about urgently needing help and felt as though I was slipping into death. I experienced a seizure. How could this have happened?

Why was my life pressing me up against a wall so hard I could barely breathe? I would have loved for someone to tell me there are not always explanations and clear-cut answers, but there is always hope and the ability to trust even when you feel utterly out of alignment. Even so, I did not crawl into a corner. I did not retreat from my life. I waited and slowly processed the experience. I was in the ICU as my babies were looked after in the NICU for the first couple days. We spent the rest of the week together in the hospital while I recovered and my blood pressure stabilized. I was confused and not sure how to do anything, but we managed, and all health issues associated with pregnancy were gone. Life with two babies is a blur for the first couple years. It was a moment-to-moment way of living. I forgot about my needs and what I wanted. All I knew is I needed to keep going and something was about to end.

After eleven years together, I told my husband I couldn't do it anymore. His mental health had taken all it could, yet he denied help, and I was exhausted in every sense of the word. I knew my life was more than motherhood. I loved it, I was honored, yet I didn't know anything else about who I was. I knew my emotions were not in alignment with my life because this was not the first time my spirit had embarked on a journey in the darkness. Alone, anxious, lost. Those were the comfortable seats that I had taken before, but never again. I could not step into my power and grow as a person in this relationship as his wife.

I decided I would take responsibility for my emotional power. I felt strength and courage, the bright light inside of me burning brighter than ever before. In a very short time, I welcomed an expansive and remarkable change. I allowed my emotions to come to the surface and pour out. I was grateful for every single one. Sadness, fear, happiness, strength, and so many more. I was separated from my husband. I was finding my truth, listening to my spirit and learning about myself, taking time to hear and feel what I needed. I needed to heal, and I asked for help. I knew life was worth living; I deserved to find out why I exist in this lifetime. Feeling love and happiness, I was learning, was my birthright.

I believed in myself, understanding that I was worth the love that I felt in my heart. I finally understood that I was love. It wasn't something that had to come from the outside first. As I started to feel love for myself, gratitude and empathy, my outlook and my experiences changed. I changed. I made hard decisions without fear; I made them with love. Seeing the good that would come of it. Maybe not right away, but one day. I trusted that I was safe, that I was guided and did what was best for me, not in a selfish way, but in a way that made me feel ultimately connected to myself. My relationship with myself and my intuition grew, I found my path and purpose, and I finalized my divorce. I started digging into what healing was and found Reiki. I am continually making choices based on authenticity now. I learn more about myself, about life, and about my intuition. My ability to experience life head on with emotional strength grows with my connection to self. My approach is to have an open heart, not to say that every day is perfect, but my reaction or lack thereof is what enables me to trust my intuitive nature.

Before writing this chapter, about a week prior, my fiancé and I had a miscarriage. It was the most emotionally powerful experience of my life. At first I wasn't sure what was happening as I had never had a miscarriage before. I knew that I could not control the outcome of whatever was happening, so I was gentle with myself. It felt like planning for a big day without any support, but more so, I was managing my expectations and then I let them all go and trusted. I trusted that what I felt in my heart, the love, the sadness, the confusion, was all meant to be. I've learned that life provides opportunity, even disguised as twisted torment. I was not devastated nor broken inside. I aligned with my higher self and knew that this was part of my life. I want you to know that you can feel this powerful alignment too. It is within you. I drove myself to the hospital and wanted it that way. I had no idea what the process was, how I would feel, what would or could happen. I drew every bit of strength I had within me, and I felt like I was in control in a situation that simply does not allow it. I calmed my mind, and I was leading with my heart. My emotions never peaked in any sense of the word. I was so focused that I was relaxed, as much as my body would allow me. I never once let my ego write a story that was going to take me somewhere I didn't want to go. I was not leaving that path I was on, I was choosing my direction, as foggy as I might have been. I wanted to feel everything—the pain, the comfort, the unknown. I did. I did it while clinging to the depth of my heart and with more preparation than ever to face my life and everything meant for me. Becoming a Reiki Master has taught me about energy and the power behind purposeful intention. Life's essence is made up of many things, but only intent can give you true feedback of what is felt in fulfillment.

Emotions and intuition have taught me that goals and visions in life seem to sustain us, minding the gap between here and there. Though when you look at life and break it down into moments, the clarity becomes crystal clear: presence is a gift. Use each and every moment you can to learn about who you are and trust that luminous space inside that lights up as you live the next experience, the next feeling. It will guide you.

Chapter 3

The Labor of Cultivating Compassion

Jennifer Leigh

Jennifer Leigh is a calming, compassionate soul with a passion for facilitating healing in the physical body through body, heart, and mind alignment. From a very young age she had the gift of healing touch and drew those who felt left out or different into her comforting space. She graduated from Johnson County Community College in 2003 with an associate degree. She's always had a passion for writing and used her gift to journal in a blog about her beautiful, creative children. After her divorce, she immediately enrolled at Wellspring School of Allied Health to fulfill her lifelong dream of becoming a licensed massage therapist. She is a certified body/mind coach, which allows her to combine her love of coming alongside clients for emotional healing with her intuitive bodywork skills that include Reiki, Myofascial Release, Deep Tissue, Reflexology, Craniosacral Therapy, and Young Living essential oils therapy. Jennifer has the gift of holding space for transformation. As much as she is gentle, she is also a powerful force with insurmountable capacities for strength, wisdom, and grace. She helps others by drawing out their strengths while gently opening the door for introspective thought on one's weaknesses. She hosts quarterly women's retreats to hold space for healing transformation and continues to collaborate with women and men in the health and wellness field.

Jennifer Leigh

@Topshelf_hippie

"You cannot force healing, gratitude, or forgiveness. The power is in the process."

For as long as I could remember, I hated myself. Since the first time I was violated as a child, I had dissociated from my body and detached from my self-worth. I was stripped of my dignity and my right to take up space in the world. I also had a father-wound of abandonment and neglect, and I looked to everyone else for my identity. I loved hard and sought approval through loving others, and still it would never fill that emotional void in me that was left by abandonment and dissociating. Because of the trauma and the family environment I grew up in, my entire life had been built on a false belief system that said, "You have no voice, you must earn the right to take up space by pleasing everyone around you. You are a burden, your needs are not important, you are unlovable, your value is determined by others, you are incompetent, you will never be enough, and you are undeserving of love." The repeated violation by men through my childhood and adolescence confirmed this belief system constructed from my father-wound, and I attracted men into my life who reflected my pain and who validated those beliefs over and over again until I was dying on the inside.

Before my healing, I would have told my life story in a much different way with bitterness and resentment, but today I stand before you with a story of redemption through forgiveness and acceptance. My life now tells the story of cultivating compassion. It's not a pretty story; it is a story filled with pain, anger, bitterness, hatred, and abuse. But what I would come to finally appreciate, and in fact be grateful for, is that it would all become the backdrop of darkness that only served to make the illumination of my inner Light that much brighter.

My spiritual awakening began when I realized that I was slowly dying of survival. I was in an unconscious marriage, my body was revolting against me as I pushed through undiagnosed chronic pain, I was in a deep depression hidden behind a fake smile, and I had completely lost myself in all of the roles I played trying to prove my worth: stay-at-home mother, trophy wife, youth leader, devoted friend, school volunteer, housekeeper, and fitness instructor, to name a few. I was giving everything I had in order to earn love and was silently attracting people and circumstances that were a reflection of my pain.

When I got divorced after being with my husband since eighteen years of age, I felt discarded and rejected, and I walked away feeling like a worthless piece of shit. My marriage would have ended sooner, but I was terrified to leave the illusion of security to try and find out who I was outside of who I allowed everyone else to tell me I was. I had to confront the death of my marriage, the death of what I thought my life was supposed to look like, and the death of the part I thought I was supposed to play in life. My recovery would depend on me recognizing that my life was built on choices I made through the false belief system that was failing me. Because of these false beliefs established by abuse, I feared abandonment by men, I feared being a burden, I feared not being enough for my husband, I feared rejection. My worst fears confirmed,

I felt helpless and paralyzed.

After my divorce, I knew that I needed to find employment, so I enrolled in massage therapy school, as this was a dream of mine for a very long time. I had always had the gift of touch, strong hands that could sense energy, and an intuition that I couldn't understand until I went through the massage therapy program. The effects that I had on people in my sessions were magical, and I knew I had tapped into a gift and skill that was divinely inspired. I had a highly sensitive intuition that had always simmered under the surface of my daily life since I was a child, but I had silenced it in an effort to keep the status quo. I always felt different from those around me, seeing things and knowing things that I could never communicate because I thought people would think I was crazy. I learned that I am a clairsentient, which means I can feel other people's energy and emotions through presence and touch, but because I had no defined boundaries that separated what my energy was and what was theirs, I took on all of the emotions of the people around me, especially those who reflected my own wounds. Through my schooling, I learned so much about this gift and came to understand how taking on others' energy because I was ungrounded had caused me to feel so much more pain and depression. After my divorce, it would take four years of blindly feeling around in the darkness searching for myself and my purpose in this world to finally hit rock bottom. It was this searching in the dark that led me to the suicidal undercurrent I had felt since I was raped for the first time as a teenager. The darkness took over and I decided to give up.

Because being a mother had been my greatest purpose and joy, I knew I had reached the darkest moment of my life when I decided that my three children would be better off without me. It was November 2016, and I had been through a lot that year between getting off prescription antidepressants, having emergency surgery, leaving a paid employee position to start my own business, being in a car accident, having overwhelming financial stress, facing the toxic political climate with the presidential elections, and having to coparent in a contentious relationship with a man who I still deeply resented. I felt like I was doing all of it all alone. I lost twenty-five pounds that month and my body was fighting bacterial infections throughout. I was literally dying on the inside when I had decided that death was my only escape from the pain. But deep inside of me there was still a small voice that said, "Hold on for one more day." So, on that Tuesday before Thanksgiving when the darkness became too much to bear, I took enough psychoactive sedatives to knock me out to keep me from following through with my suicide plan. I knew my children were coming home the next day, and if I could hold on until then, I could make it through the holiday surrounded by family. I held on, and as a last-ditch effort to survive, I checked myself into a psychiatric hospital. It would take me a long time to recognize just how strong and brave I was that day, but I'm grateful for that moment I chose life.

It was a surreal moment to have to walk into that hospital with my mom, not knowing what would happen, when I'd be released, what the treatment would be like, or if it would even be successful. I just knew that I needed a safe place to let go, with no responsibility, no mask to wear, nothing to prove, stripped down to the basics of life. I felt so empty, so exhausted, so desperate, so broken; I felt numb, dead inside. I needed to let go of trying to hold it all together. This was what my rock bottom looked like.

In that hospital I met other women who were feeling the same way I was. I could feel and see that familiar pain in their bodies, and my heart ached. I was attuned to their pain and I found myself engaging with them with compassion and understanding. They felt seen and heard and understood through our interactions, and I was validated in my pain knowing I wasn't alone. Little did I know when I hit this rock bottom that I was in store for a complete system reboot. In order to get that reboot, I needed to *feel* again, to get pissed enough to want my life to change. Anger is a very powerful motivator. I was angry that these other women were treated the way they were, that they saw themselves as pathetic, worthless, unlovable, and broken. I saw myself in them, and after a few days of numbness in that stale and sterile gray mental hospital, a flame sparked as that small voice inside of me screamed, "Fight for me!" Numbness turned to anger, and I wanted to get the hell out of there. It felt like a prison; I had physically manifested my internal prison, and I was smacked in the face with the reality that I could choose to remain in that prison or I could listen to that inner voice that said, "You were made for more than this!" My whole life I had been searching for someone to rescue me, but for the first time in my life I connected with a part of me that said, "Only you have the power to rescue yourself."

At my core I knew I was a loving, caring, generous, giving, kind woman, but I couldn't see any of that buried under my emotional pain and the pain of others. It wasn't until I understood what an empath was that I realized that I had spent my whole life allowing myself to absorb other people's negative energy and emotions while never fully releasing my own emotions. I was holding it all and drowning in it. Slowly, I became aware of how my emotional trauma had controlled how I saw and experienced the world. I was this completely open emotional being who had taken everything as a personal reflection of who I was, and I let it weigh me down like a sunken ship. Doing the work and getting out of that hell was just as painful as getting into it, but like the alchemical process of turning coal into diamonds, it was worth every single moment. I am a Lightworker who experienced deep pain, and I chose to transmute that pain to help heal our collective consciousness through awakening, release, and reprogramming of the unconscious. All Lightworkers require this alchemical process in order to clear their energy field and become a channel for facilitating healing. I call it the labor of cultivating compassion. It was time to start purging that energy and living life believing that I am the woman I really am underneath it all. I began an unfolding process that would last a few years and bring along more pain as I burned, scraped, and shook off what no longer served my highest good. I surrendered and received. I cleared out and rebuilt.

The spiritual journey is not for the faint of heart. It takes intense bravery and courage to face your fears, your deepest wounds, your darkest spaces. And not only face them, but EMBRACE them. The journey was not to "fix" myself; I was not broken. The journey was to INTEGRATE myself and find all those fragmented parts that I had hidden away, covered, built walls around, and excommunicated. The parts that were shamed, violated, abused, neglected, and abandoned were all there carrying the unprocessed emotions and memories from trauma.

I read books on self-worth, I listened to guided meditations that helped me connect to my divinity, I went through programs that helped me understand and heal from narcissistic abuse, I sought wise counsel from therapists and friends who listened to and saw my pain as well as my Light. This journey required that I find and embrace each fragmented part of myself and love and accept it, approve and validate it. I embraced the child who was sexually molested in daycare, traumatically separated from her body because it wasn't safe. I embraced the young girl who never received the love, protection, and attention from her father, which kept her from seeing that she was valuable and worthy. I embraced that fifteen-year-old girl who was raped by five boys, who lay there lifeless while she was violated, paralyzed by fear wondering what she had done to deserve this humiliation and abuse. I embraced the young woman who handed her power over to a man who used her for seventeen years and discarded her when she no longer served his purpose. I spoke truth to her: that she didn't deserve to be treated that way, that she was worthy of using her voice to speak up and defend herself, that she was loved and worthy of love. Like a mother holds her child, I tenderly held all those fragmented parts that suffered abuse at the hands of strangers, people who claimed to love me, and ultimately, my own self. I assured myself that I am whole and safe now and, regardless of how I was treated before, that I am so very loved.

In this process I learned that forgiveness continues to be the key to my healing. Forgiveness is not about the other person, it is about me releasing myself from pain. And forgiveness cannot be "done," it must be "allowed." The key to allowing is releasing the need for an apology or needing the offense to not have happened in the first place, and this starts with acceptance. I accepted that I had been victimized. I accepted that I had shamed myself for being victimized, and I accepted that I hurt others from that place of shame. Forgiveness was a gift for myself. When I was able to consciously acknowledge and accept this fact, I forgave myself for hurting others when I was in pain. I forgave myself for not knowing what I didn't know. I forgave myself for not leaving a toxic marriage when I saw the signs. I forgave myself for staying in that marriage out of fear and desperation. I forgave myself for handing my power over to everyone else. When I accept and forgive myself, I am able to let go of the hurt, knowing that the people who hurt me were only projecting the pain they were in while reflecting the pain I was in. Forgiveness transmutes fear, anger, resentment, and bitterness into the only real thing in this world: love. And love heals you. This love shifted me into a space of compassion. I released those people who victimized me. I no longer needed anything from them, and I was freed.

Unfortunately, you cannot force healing, forgiveness, or gratitude. The power is in the process. I've spent the last few years learning to give myself grace and compassion throughout this process. I've realized that the answer to every problem I have is self-compassion. I've learned to set boundaries so that I don't take on others' emotions. I learned that all of my emotions are valid and that if I allow myself to accept and feel every emotion that comes through, not rejecting it or pushing it away, I can remain in control of my actions when I get emotional and let them pass through me. I've learned the importance of staying embodied through the body-mind connection and not disconnecting or fragmenting from my body. I am repatterning my behavior to reflect love instead of fear. Today, I accept myself wholly, including the parts of me that are still hurting and holding hatred and bitterness.

My new foundational belief system is built on truth: I am loved. I am worthy. I am enough. I will no longer look to someone else to define and validate me. I am in control of my emotions. I get to decide who I am and who I will become based on self-compassion and truth. I am safe and supported by Love because I am love. I am ecstasy, I am joy, I am freedom. I am abundance. I am what I have been looking for. I no longer need a rescuer to heal my wounds and make me whole because I embraced both the Light and the Shadow within, and I courageously rescued myself.

~ Thank you to my mom, Cheryl, for being a rock and a light with love in my life. Thank you to my three beautiful children, Mason, Mya, and Makenna, who embody all that is good in me and survived all that was shattered. Thank you to Angela for all your support and encouragement and for being my loving and wise guide on this journey. Thank you to Brad for pushing me and reflecting masculine energy while holding a safe, strong space for me to let go and explore my divinity. Thank you to Cassie for this priceless opportunity to share my story in hopes that others will feel the Light and hope. Thank you to my friends and family who saw beauty inside of me when I only saw darkness . . . I love you all.

Jennifer Leigh

Chapter 4

Reparenting the Inner Child

Rose Finlay

After a catastrophic injury at the age of seventeen that left her a quadriplegic, Rose Finlay has continued to push the boundaries of societal norms and expectations surrounding disability. A mama to three little dudes and a successful entrepreneur and disability advocate, her unstoppable spirit and ferociously positive outlook inspire her to chase her lifelong goals despite the challenges of being a quadriplegic and recovering from an autoimmune condition. As a holistic health practitioner and empowerment mentor, Rose has found purpose and the drive to remain committed to her own personal growth and development.

Stepping confidently into her next venture as an accessibility consultant, she is eager to help bridge the gaps between disabled communities and equal access to opportunity.

Embracing her power and personal freedom, Rose finally allowed herself to step into her truth. She took full ownership for her individuality and found ways to overcome the dialogue of internalized ableism. "They can't see you if you hide your light."

This spiritually grounded mama is passionate about raising her littles while striving to be a consistent example of gratitude, mindfulness, and empathy. This shining light pours inspiration into all the cracks in your soul while evoking a strong belief in self.

Rose Finlay

www.rosefinlay.ca

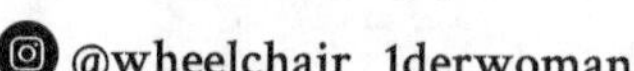
@wheelchair_1derwoman

Rose Finlay

"Consciousnesses and intuition are two of the greatest superpowers given to humankind. Don't waste them."

From birth until the time we leave this earthly form, we are continuously exploring what is external input and what is our internal knowledge. Our surroundings, our emotions and responses are all interconnected, but what's entirely separate is our intuition. Our ability to interpret and trust intuition can be greatly affected by the above factors.

In childhood we are taught rules and expectations—by parents, in social settings, and by the outside world at large. There are expectations surrounding religion, education, career, marriage, and children. We are expected, to a certain extent, to follow the path led by our parents and family members before us. It is our childhood programming and social conditioning. This tradition of following in the footsteps of our ancestors used to make more sense when the herd mentality was necessary for survival.

My childhood was anything but "normal" after my mother's sudden death. My parents had already been separated and going through a less than amicable divorce. My parents were an incredibly volatile couple.

They both possessed a strong energy, uncompromising opinions and very different perspectives, but in many ways were so much alike.

My brothers and I had been living primarily with our mother until the tragic accident that ended her life at the age of thirty-two. My oldest brother was from my mother's previous relationship, and my younger brother and I shared the same father. The decision was made that we would be living with our fathers, which meant my older brother would be living about forty-five minutes from us.

Living with my father after my mother's passing proved not to be a viable option. My father's struggles with mental health and addictions were not conducive to raising small children, especially children who were processing their own trauma. I instinctively became very protective of my younger brother. We were raised mainly by my aunt and uncle, who had no kids of their own. We spent time living apart from them at different times throughout our childhood and teenage years, staying with other relatives for a myriad of reasons.

As a child who experienced such trauma at a young age, I learned very unhealthy coping mechanisms for grief and loss. My aunt and uncle had different ways of parenting than both my mother and father. Different doesn't necessarily mean bad, it was just unfamiliar. My aunt and uncle were able to provide a far more stable home life, which I am eternally grateful for. I always knew my life was entirely different from that of my peers. I felt very much like the black sheep.

As a spiritual person now, I'm grateful for all of the hard parts of my journey. I have a much different understanding of why these painful lessons are necessary. Having multiple parental figures and different sources of input into my childhood programming gave me the opportunity to interpret my own morality.

With my father's lack of involvement, I felt orphaned. His tumultuous lifestyle made me vow from a young age to create a healthy family of my own. I established a "Do It Yourself" mindset and had trust issues from such a young age. I wasn't born into a family that filled my needs for nurturing and genuine love, and this mindset was my solution to fill that need. I was determined to create what I felt would fill that void.

My father's absence deeply instilled the belief that I wasn't enough. I wasn't valuable enough for him to want to be engaged. Keep in mind that these are the thoughts of a child with no understanding of mental illness and substance abuse.

I suffered a cervical spinal cord injury at the age of seventeen. A catastrophic injury that forever changed my life. Another major traumatic life event that I understandably struggled with processing for many years that only added to my insecurities and increased my feelings of inadequacy. It added significant complexities to my daily life and my family's overall dysfunction. My injury was another unimaginable loss for me. One that is never easy for anyone who sustains a spinal cord injury. I went from being an independent teenager with a thirst for adventure and learning to being dependent on my family for all my basic daily needs. I was angry and resentful. I was confused and scared. I didn't know how to accept life in a different capacity. When I was first injured, the doctors were very direct with my family about how fragile my life and overall health in general were now that I was a quadriplegic.

"Fatal complications of spinal cord injury include blood clots and sepsis due to pneumonia, urinary infections or pressure sores."[1]

As much as I disagreed with what the doctors said, there was a part of my subconscious that absorbed the notion that my health was fragile. I didn't buy into the idea of not recovering, I knew my body was more capable than they thought. I also refused to let anyone else dictate my story. I fluxed over the years on where I pushed the boundaries and where I let fear control my decisions. I took chances, I traveled, I lived. I did a lot of the things that I was told I may never do again. I hadn't forgotten the teen with an innate longing for knowledge, truth, and adventure.

Having children of my own is what changed things the most. It brought back so much of my unprocessed childhood trauma and many insecurities.

I arrived at a place in my late twenties where all this programming was detrimental to my own mental health and well-being. My thoughts and beliefs were not in alignment with what I innately FELT.

At twenty-seven, I was a (mostly) stay-at-home mom to three beautiful little boys. My youngest son was less than a year old. I had just taken the leap back into the business world with my passion for natural wellness as my driving force. I found myself within a business network that had the alluring promise of community and support, something I was craving after feeling so isolated while at home raising babies for the previous five years. Needless to say, I didn't find what I was looking for. I didn't feel the sense of belonging that I had been looking for. I didn't realize it then but this emptiness, this lonely feeling, wasn't the result of stay-at-home life. It was a feeling that I had carried along with me since childhood.

I found myself in my third failing marriage, overwhelmed by surmounting debt and struggling with my lack of identity. I couldn't understand how my determination to create the family life I needed as a child had instead created this storm of chaos. I also realized then that

I had been using the identity of wife, mother, and business owner to escape the responsibility of my own emotional healing.

I decided that I needed to give myself the space to explore these feelings, which started first with my home life. I needed to take a break spiritually from my marriage. My husband and I continued living together and parenting our children, but I knew that in order for me to be able to do the necessary "soul work," I needed to step away from my role as a wife. To be clear, this in no way meant that I was looking for another partner. The opposite, actually. I knew that I needed to find my way back to myself, not anyone else.

My marriage was riddled with unresolved conflict, conflict that I had exhausted myself trying to reconcile. The lack of trust created anxiety and eventually anxiety became fear. Marriage often comes with a whole lot of expectations. Having unrealistic expectations is a surefire way to feel disappointed. The less in control I felt, the more control I tried to grasp. I needed to find peace in my mind in order to get a clear understanding of how to feel secure and trust my own thoughts. In order for it to be possible for me to hear this message of intuitive knowing, I needed to quiet the chaos. I had to truly listen to my soul's communication to know what exactly was required for my reality to be in alignment with my higher self.

It's easy to lose yourself in toxic relationships. Whether or not you realize it or are willing to acknowledge it, we lose a certain level of autonomy in relationships. In a healthy relationship, both partners try their absolute best to understand each other's views and opinions. In a toxic relationship, one or both partners try to imprint their beliefs on the other. This can become alarmingly dangerous because it has the ability to interfere with one's ability to listen to their own intuition.

This was a breaking point for me. My life as I knew it had become unbearable, unlivable even. I didn't feel fully connected to my spiritual beliefs until I had no choice but to have blind faith in my own ability to heal my body, mind, and soul.

I changed the way I thought, the way I spoke to myself and others, the way I carried myself. I also changed what I studied and the books I read. I stopped watching the news, I stopped judging. I started loving, meditating, and praying. I started to truly take care of myself instead of being so concerned with pleasing others.

Growing up without the foundation that I so desperately needed left me with many deficits. I had learned unhealthy coping mechanisms rather than self-regulation. My DIY mindset reinforced my fierce independence that stemmed from feeling unsupported and misunderstood in my younger years. I lacked the ability to ask for help and trust that the people around me could be there to provide that support.

Now that I was responsible for the well-being of my three sweet little people, I became determined to reparent myself and learn self-mastery, not only for myself but to ensure that the toxic coping mechanisms that I learned were not what I passed down to my own children. The control that I was so desperately seeking externally was a blaring indication that I was completely out of control internally. I was done repeating these painful cycles. I didn't like feeling like I needed to do things all on my own.

As I began to make the significant and necessary changes in my life, things began to feel easier. My anxious thoughts began to fade. I no longer felt like a victim to my circumstances. I needed to feel all the things that I had been avoiding in order to shift from my survival skills to living incongruently with my soul.

Healing in itself is its own journey. An adventure of sorts to find out who we really are at the core of our being. This adventure is very individual and is triggered by different life events. It's easy to fall into the habit of (consciously or subconsciously) remaining in a constant state of busy in order to avoid doing the self-reflecting needed in order to comprehend the lesson. There is always a lesson. If we look at life as a continuous learning experience, the possibilities for expansion and growth are endless. It is often our ego that impedes this. When we step into the role of "forever student" at the school of life, we open ourselves to opportunities we hadn't even considered before. This alone has the ability to empower and encourage people to continue looking for ways to expand their own consciousness. Ego, at its root, is a defense mechanism. It's also a huge hindrance on the journey to self. When we begin to quiet the ego by turning inward, we allow the voice of intuition to speak more clearly.

Sometimes the painful parts of our life are the most valuable, not the most important, but they provide insight that otherwise would never occur to us. I didn't understand earlier in my life how vital these traumatic events would be in my own conscious awakening. We find ourselves either living by the rules of our childhood programming or we override the default setting and live by intuition. There is a certain level of comfort and safety in living by the default setting, the expectations set out for us by others. Choosing to create our own standards and set boundaries can definitely make waves within relationships, families, and even communities. Setting clear boundaries is an imperative step in protecting one's ability to truly and deeply tune into their intuition. As soon as we begin to allow others to violate these boundaries, we are giving away that personal power.

Through meditation and self-reflection I have been able to achieve a level of self-mastery that allows me to be much less reactive to things that once triggered me. I was hyperreactive to my environment because

I had unprocessed trauma. I became much more diligent with my morning rituals. I sat in stillness and quieted my mind. In this space I was able to ask myself the hard questions: "Why am I reacting this way?" "Why am I hurt by this?" "Is this worth my personal peace?" I did a lot of journaling. Somedays, I would write for hours. It was a peaceful reprieve from frantically thinking about my next move or how I was going to rebuild my life. Letting go of everything you know comes with a new level of fear and uncertainty, but I knew with every part of my being that this was the only way to find my way back to myself. After taking the time to focus on the soul work, I found myself to be much more understanding of and easy with my tender soul. I had to remove all the armor, the unhealthy coping mechanisms, and essentially drop ego from the equation. I had to find my inner child and start from scratch, giving myself the love, understanding, and acceptance that I needed as a child. I feel like reparenting is now a lifelong process. It's important to let things happen the way they need to. Feel the feelings. Lean into the lessons. We only have one shot at this thing called life. Learning to forgive ourselves, be accountable to self, and practice self-love are such essential steps to awakening.

You won't know what your soul has in store for you until you have the courage to listen. The courage to question all the beliefs you were raised with. My life now in comparison to three years ago is much more peaceful. I'm not attracting repetitive toxic cycles and relationships. I don't tolerate being treated poorly. I know who I am and where my personal boundaries are. I don't settle.

It's important to appreciate your roots and honor the journey. You are not condemned by your past. You have the choice to rise from the ashes and heal your wounds, creating something entirely new for yourself and generations after you. Be brave.

~ To my three incredible little people, thank you for choosing me to be your mama. You have been the candle of hope through the dark night of my soul. You give me the strength to courageously battle my demons. To my aunt and uncle, I am forever grateful for your selfless love and support. To the incredible people who have become my soul family on this path to reparenting, your love and input in my life is such a treasured gift from the divine. There are no words to describe my deep feelings of pure gratitude, but I hope that I lead a life that demonstrates how much your love has made an impact on me.

Rose Finlay

Chapter 5

A Message from the Bees

Jasmine Cabanaw

Jasmine Cabanaw is an award-winning writer with expertise in history, international development, and communications. She is the founder of Green Bamboo Publishing, a company that publishes children's books based on rescue animals. Her next project involves studying physics, psychology, and neurology in order to understand the science behind how she cured herself from fibromyalgia. Jasmine has set a goal to write a book about the experience in order to bring this knowledge to the world and help people who suffer from chronic pain.

Jasmine Cabanaw

@jasminejunec / @greenbamboopublishing

Jasmine June C / Green Bamboo Publishing

I've learned that profound things are possible—even miracles—for those who believe in the power of love.

The most powerful love I ever experienced was in the middle of a vortex of bees. Throughout my life I had struggled with the conventional definition of love until I realized it didn't matter what name I gave the constant force that was in my life—unconditional love, divine love, self-love, romantic love—it's all the same emotion from the same Source. The bees ultimately taught me that.

That said, I'm not going to pretend to have all the answers. I'm simply going to share the chain of events that led me to embrace my own power and which enabled me to heal myself from a chronic pain disease called fibromyalgia, a disease that had me suffering for most of my life—stiff joints, brain fog, aching muscles, and skin so sensitive and painful to touch that I sometimes couldn't even wear clothes without being in agony. Fibromyalgia has no cure—or so I was told.

My journey to true healing began when a series of events prompted me to start meditating again. I had forgotten what tapping into that higher vibration could do for me. It was an important lesson because it made me wonder if I had forgotten about other positive things from my past. I decided to pursue the benefits that were emerging from meditation, and over the course of six months I gradually increased my daily meditation practice from ten minutes to a minimum of one hour. The synchronicities in my life immediately started to increase.

The first significant one was the day I started going to the free yoga class at the beautiful cathedral down the road from me. It was one of the few places where I could be injured and still do yoga—even if all I did was sit on the mat. The day before I had been reminiscing about working with children, and I put a wish out into the Universe for an opportunity to come my way so that I could volunteer with children again. I was feeling a little helpless because of my illness and wanted to find a way to still make a positive contribution to society. That very night at yoga, a member from an organization that connects children in foster care with mentors presented after class. I took that synchronicity as a sign, enrolled in the program immediately, and fell back in love with trusting my intuition.

Soon after I made that decision the Universe gave me another gift. I had taken the day to myself, to just wander the streets of San Francisco, to heal and reflect. At the beginning of my walk I thought about the wild parrots that had long made their home in the city and how I hadn't seen any in a while. Wouldn't it be nice to see them that day, especially when I was feeling so sad?

At the end of my walk I came back to that place where I'd thought about the parrots, and as I approached, a cacophony of parrot voices filled the streets. Usually the flocks contain a couple dozen at most, but that day there were over a hundred. It was so beautiful and magical and joyous that traffic stopped in the street. As I stood watching the birds play in the trees, a section of them branched off and flew past me, so close that I could feel their feathery wings brush my face. Sometimes a little gift, a little miracle, gives us the strength to heal and keep going.

Eventually, the combination of a breakup, my illness, and needing to heal from an accident prompted a two-month trip to Costa Rica, where I could just be in nature and continue my recovery. The magic continued to unfold and my ability to trust in myself increased.

The Universe had more gifts waiting for me. The most profound was a visit from a thousand bees. They descended upon my house in Costa Rica like tiny buzzing angels—an experience that was both beautiful and terrifying all at once. For what did I know of bees? My initial reaction was fear, but then some deep intuition took over and I knew I was not to harm these bees. They were there for a reason, and I could choose how to manage my emotions.

My mother, my nephew, and his best friend were visiting for the week. We did not know what to do about the bees, so we simply closed all the windows and doors and left. Our destination that day was the ten kilometers of trail that runs through the rainforest in Cahuita National Park. When we arrived, the entrance to the park was obvious, but my intuition was pulling me in a different direction toward a path that was off to the side. I was learning to pay attention to those gentle nudges. My nephew offered to go see what was there. He came back to report that there was a sloth hanging above the river. What a delight! We had just arrived and were already seeing a sloth. It felt like a good sign.

Three hours passed wandering through the park, my senses tantalized by the sound of crashing waves, leaves rustling in the wind, colorful explosions of flowers, the smell of wet moss and sea salt, and the delightful encounters with a plethora of wildlife. Sloths, howler monkeys, parrots, oh my! Anteaters, agouti, raccoons, bats, spider monkeys, and iguanas, too. There were so many animals, I couldn't keep track of all the ones I saw. All of this was a reminder of how everything is connected.

We arrived back from Cahuita thinking that the bees were gone. But they weren't gone, just hidden. This experience was when I discovered another benefit of meditation—quieting your mind allows you to hear things more clearly. A few days after our hike, I was meditating in the living room when I heard a strange vibrating noise coming from the wall, and when I placed my hand on it, the wall was hot! The bees were buzzing so powerfully that I could feel the vibrations before my hand even touched the surface. I wanted the bees to be safe, but they also couldn't remain in my wall. I stood there confused, not knowing what to do.

Fortunately, Costa Rica is full of good-hearted people. A friend put me in touch with a bee rescuer: Api-Agricultura. He examined the situation the next morning and happily proclaimed, "The bees can be saved! We will relocate the bees!"

I did not know what to expect from Operation Bee Rescue, and again I encountered much more than I could have possibly imagined. Once the section of the wall was removed, the bee rescuer just stared at the bees, tears welling up in his eyes. "These are the most loving bees I have ever met," he said, as he proceeded to pet the swarm of bees with his bare hand. "They are just so full of love."

He asked if I wanted to experience something incredible. Boy, did I ever! To rescue the bees, they capture the queen and put her in a bee box, which functions like an artificial hive. Once the queen is in the box, the rest of the bees leave their hive in a flurry and join her. Usually it is not recommended to be near the box when this is happening, but the bee rescuer said that these bees were different, they were so full of love that it would be safe. "If you stand over the box and show no fear," he said, "you will get the chance to be in the middle of a thousand bees."

How do I describe that energy, that feeling of thousands of tiny wings brushing against my skin, the vibration of their humming running like an electric current over my body? The vortex of bees whirled all around me, but I did not get stung. After all the bees were snug in their box, I stepped back, exhilarated and breathless. I would be forever changed, knowing that choosing love over fear had allowed me to experience that miracle.

After that, bees started showing up in my life wherever I went. The first time I met the foster child I was to mentor, she introduced herself, looked at me quizzically and said, "Can I show you the bees? I feel like showing you the bees in the garden for some reason." Things like that happened time and time again.

There was a reason both my conscious and subconscious mind were paying attention to these moments. The combination of paying attention to my fears, letting go of past trauma, and embracing my inner power was instrumental in helping me heal from fibromyalgia. I spent hours in deep meditation, doing relentless self-reflection and self-hypnosis, and spiraling into the depths of my own soul. I reconnected with my own concept of "God" in a way that felt pure, spiritual, and full of love.

Focusing on my own power, emotions, and vibrations helped me realize that I, too, was like the bees—a being of perfect, divine love. Then one day I went into deep meditation and fully let go, and when I came out of the trance, all the fibromyalgia symptoms were gone. My body felt so different. I could feel the electric current of my energy running through every cell of my body—a powerful energy, capable of healing me from trauma and disease. An energy that allowed me to embrace the full power of my mind.

As I awakened to this reality more and more, I finally saw the truth about the bees—the bees were not just for me. The bees were for everyone because, like a hive, we were all connected.

If I needed proof, I only had to look at how these magnificent creatures operate. They are the most mathematically perfect species in the world. Their home is so geometrically perfect and structurally sound that engineers are using honeycombs as a model for homes on Mars. Their society functions so that everyone has a place, with the queen fully supported by the entire hive. Bees vote by dancing. The bees start dancing in squiggly figure eights, and when all the bees are unanimously dancing in the same direction, the decision has been made. The queen is thought to represent the divine feminine, and while she leads, the worker bees are just as important because the survival of the hive depends mostly on them. All the bees have a prominent role and their connection to one another is what keeps their hive alive. In almost every religion, bees are cited as messengers of God. That's how sacred they are.

When I think back to all the times I've encountered bees in my life, I realize that they've always been there, I just wasn't consciously aware. It is the same with love and the power of my own mind. If I open my eyes and look inside myself, I find the miracle of the entire Universe is there. The power of my infinite energy has existed all along, just waiting to shine, even during times when the world was dark. Currently, there is not an ounce of hate in my heart. There is also not a trace of fibromyalgia symptoms in my body—I am free from the bondage of pain that had plagued me since my childhood. I have fully embraced the divine magic of unconditional love.

The newness and the sheer miracle of healing from fibromyalgia at first caused me to think it was a purely spiritual event. I think this is a normal reaction to an abrupt change in reality, especially one you had been told was impossible. After I adjusted to this new way of being, I decided to look beyond the magic of the experience and see if there was science to support it.

I was fortunate that my history degree and years in the marketing industry had provided me with robust research skills. After several months of thorough research, I discovered I was not the only one who had experienced a miracle. Despite being classified as an incurable illness, there are numerous people who have healed from fibromyalgia. All these people had healed through a similar means as I had. There are doctors who have whole programs designed to cure fibromyalgia—and with enough successful cases that the evidence is starting to pile up.

The science hasn't quite uncovered just how everything is connected, but the evidence shows a relationship between the ancillary nervous system and the way our minds and bodies experience pain. The fields of physics and neuroscience in particular are starting to prove that the energy within our minds is capable of producing physical effects. Some of this information was already obvious and well known, but scientists are learning that our minds are even more capable of affecting our bodies than we thought. The reason meditation and self-hypnosis can create an opportunity for healing is because they allow conscious thoughts to register on a subconscious and unconscious level, which is where healing takes place. For example, when you cut your finger, you don't consciously tell your finger to heal—your unconscious mind takes care of that.

Understanding this information, that there was science to support the miracle I experienced, strengthened the trust I had in myself because it validated my intuition. The subconscious mind communicates in pictures, stories, symbols, and obscure words. The conscious mind often struggles to put the correct words to this sign language. And that is where trusting yourself comes in. It is not easy to decipher these messages, especially when we don't understand the emotions that are attached to them.

I now see emotions as tools, and if I know how to wield them wisely, I can have a whole arsenal of emotions available in my tool kit. My most favorite of these is love, but I have also uncovered the benefits of some of the more difficult emotions, such as anger and grief.

Plus, if life ever gets too difficult and I start to have doubts, if I ever need a little extra help, I know I can just follow the bees. Those beautiful tiny messengers—like so many others—are here to show me the way. I just have to be aware and pay attention and embrace the vibrations of love. I've learned that profound things are possible—even miracles—for those who believe in the power of love. Pay attention to the synchronicities in your own life, and if you desire, embrace the power of your own divinity. Who knows what miracles may await?

Chapter 6

Wake the Wild Within

Olivia Shwetz

Olivia Shwetz is the intuitive light within her communities both online and offline. Known for having the loudest laugh in the room, her personality exudes positivity! She easily gives others the permission they need to shine brighter. Olivia inspires others to awaken to their wild within, all while embracing even the darkest parts of themselves. Hence the name of her business, "Wake the Wild Within," established in 2018. Her own life has evidence that one can choose to walk powerfully through any of life's challenges. She has experienced grief, celebration, laughter, sorrow, and anger, and she has learned how to surrender to it all with a grateful heart. Olivia believes that life is always happening for you, not to you. With this philosophy, it's no wonder she has gracefully overcome the challenges the universe has sent her way: bouts of depression, losing beloved people to suicide, overcoming anxiety, unexpected pregnancy, and more, all which have led her down a winding path but have ultimately brought her to where she is now. Olivia has stepped into her soul-aligned role as a Spiritual Advisor. With her intuitive gifts, she helps others open up to the possibility within them. By making spiritual self-care a priority in her life, she knows how vital it is to others to absorb this practice into theirs. Olivia is always looking for ways to help others stand in their truth in a way that serves them because she believes that it is everyone's divine right to live a full life! It's also every individual's responsibility to embrace themselves fully and trust the wild within. We all have darkness that can be transmuted into light and awaken to our power. She believes that everyone needs to develop their intuition and learn to trust their inner wild wholeheartedly.

Olivia Shwetz

www.wakethewildwithin.com

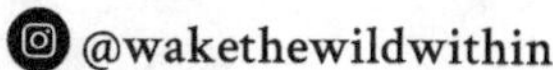

@wakethewildwithin

wakethewildwithin

"Do not fear the wild that has always been inside. Wake it, recognize it, and harness the power of your soul. You are meant to do great things."

There's an old Cherokee story[1] about two wolves that live within each person, constantly at battle with one another. One is Dark—full of anger, envy, sorrow, false pride, superiority, arrogance, ego, guilt, regret, greed, resentment. The other is Light—full of joy, peace, love, hope, serenity, humility, kindness, benevolence, empathy, truth, compassion, generosity. How does the battle end? Which will win?

Both wolves exist and there is no denying their presence. They are woven into our subconscious, our heart of hearts, and yet many of us aren't conscious of their primal pulls, to the inner battle. It's not until we truly awaken that we become aware of the fight between the two and how it impacts our life. Just as there is a yin, there is a yang. There is light and dark, a "good" wolf and a "bad" wolf, each vying to win inside us all. Which one wins? Who's in control? Sit back and take a moment to collect yourself. Which one is your current emotional state resonating with in you at this moment?

I wasn't conscious of these inner wolves until later on in life, but growing up, I was always drawn to wolves in general. I'm sure when I was younger it was because they were the closest animal to a dog, but now that I look back, it's aptly due to their natural intuitive nature. Wolves have this ability to thrive in diverse environments, they realize how important the pack is to their survival, and most importantly, they trust their instincts. Nothing except for humans and tigers can bring them down. They're powerful creatures that demand respect.

In my younger years I did research papers on the different subspecies of wolves for school. I convinced my dad to change my seascape wallpaper to one of wolves. My first sewing class project was a wolf panel pillow. The first quilt I completed on my own was—you guessed it—wolves! Soon my friends gifted me wolf statues, and my high school sweetheart even drew me a beautiful wolf portrait that I still cherish today. I surrounded myself with wolves, almost as if subconsciously I knew they were guiding me to recognize my own inner "wild" and the battle within.

This inner wild is our ability to trust our instincts and eliminate the need for outside validation. The beauty of this gift is that it isn't something we learn as we grow older, it is something that inherently exists within us. This knowing, this intuition, is something that many of us forget as we age. Whether it's societal influencing, or just not a part of how we are raised, it's something I wish everyone to remember is within them. Which then begs the question, how does one remember? How does one awaken something that's long been forgotten? What does it take for someone to find their way back home to themselves?

The journey is different for everyone because though our journeys may have similarities, they are as unique as snowflakes. Some of us will be raised and taught about what it looks like to be fully awakened, while others may not ever find and recognize their own wild within. I was fortunate enough to be in my late twenties when I began to recognize what had always been inside, but it took my whole world falling apart in order for me to see clearly. It's in those moments of trauma, grief, or extreme hardship when most of us uncover our wild and take steps to harness it. Luckily, though, that doesn't have to be the case for everyone, even you.

I spent the majority of my twenties looking for that something in others, never realizing it was always within. I was never comfortable or satisfied with being on my own. I felt more secure latching on to others rather than risk standing on my own two feet. It turned me into a serial relationship hopper and someone who numbed her pain with alcohol. Looking back, I can see where the imbalances were. The moments that the dark wolf was winning the inner battle, and the rare moments the light wolf would attempt to gain ground. The times when that inner light wolf—that knowing, that intuition—would surface never lasted long before I'd either ignore it or be too riddled with doubt to trust it. We all experience moments of questioning our instincts, and unfortunately, most of what we acquire within our subconscious thinking is learned through the people who are with us as we age.

Spiritual awakenings are known to begin after a painful experience or moment of extreme trauma. Have courage to be aware of what you're going through, recognize it for what it is, and step forward fearlessly. You will not be disappointed. There is support out there for you, including an entire Universe that is ready to step up in surprising ways.

The year I connected to, and woke up something magical within me, that inner wild, was 2013. It happened after having gone through a very difficult nine months and losing someone I loved dearly. It was like hitting a rock bottom I never knew existed. Death has a strange way of reminding us of our mortality, of offering us an opportunity to put ourselves through a rebirth. It was in the months of grief that I gave myself permission to begin the painful process of dismantling everything I thought I knew about myself. It was an excruciating process, and one that would take me several years of work before I'd feel confident in who I was now consciously choosing to become. This journey was not an overnight process; it took patience and determination mixed with a lot of responsibility and radical reflection. It started extremely slowly at first, just small moments of clarity like learning to be kinder to myself and do more of what brought me joy. All of it started to happen, and small changes that I made consistently grew into second-nature habits. Love and support began to pour into my life, which was a big surprise for me because for years prior I'd felt very much alone. Through the inner work I was finally able to witness the battle within. This newfound sense of awareness helped me to consciously and confidently decide which wolf needed to lead me and when. There were days I regretted ever becoming this aware of myself and the imbalance I'd created within me because it meant I had to take responsibility. Taking responsibility isn't usually an easy task. It meant I had to do the work and show up for myself like never before. It meant changing from the inside out, and change I did.

During this process of unbecoming, it was the dismantling of my ego that proved to be the most challenging. The dark wolf within me had grown incredibly strong, therefore making it rather difficult to nurture the light wolf back into the mix. In the beginning I was convinced I had to let one of them wither away to nothingness, but too much of anything is a bad thing no matter how good it may seem. In some ways I'd allowed myself to be convinced that certain aspects of myself not only needed to be fully released, but basically destroyed for this process to be successful—to fully awaken, to feel whole. Luckily, that wasn't entirely true. I was never a bad person, but I did do bad things to good people. Hurt people, hurt people, and it's as simple as that. So when I began to heal and dismantle myself, those memories of the bad things I did became lessons and guidance for my newfound self. The biggest realization for me was that those past bad choices and experiences did not define or decide who I get to become. They will always be a part of my story, but by becoming reflective and taking responsibility, they serve me in a new and more powerful way. Remember that the future is unwritten, and the past is gone—it's up to you to choose what defines you. You always have the power to change, no matter what.

As I continued to take steps along my journey and my awareness expanded, I soon saw that everything in life is about balance. We need to ensure we're vigilant in taking care of ourselves without depleting everything we are into others. We need to ensure we eat a well-balanced diet and not indulge in bad food habits. We need to set healthy boundaries and ensure others respect our needs. We must openly communicate, not just with ourselves, but with those we love. There is courage found within vulnerability. When we take a moment to step out of our lives and into a reflective perspective, we can see where we are imbalanced—which wolf has advantage and changes the outcome.

There have been moments when I've been far too generous to a point where it was taken advantage of several times over, just as there have been moments of extreme ruthlessness that have led me to treat people terribly. All of it was part of my unbecoming, my necessary experiences to bring me to where I am today—whole, balanced, and standing in my power. It is possible to achieve, all it takes is a willingness to take an honest look at our behaviors and experiences and learn from them. I did it, you may have started doing it, or you may not quite be ready.

Throughout my life I have repeated similar situations and experiences. I'm sure you may be able to say the same upon deeper reflection.

These universal lessons are brought back around on purpose to give us an opportunity to learn, to see the lesson, and grow. Funny how that works, right? We go through a similar situation over and over again. Sometimes with the same results, and other times we gain the awareness to shift and that gives us a different outcome. Usually one that finally puts that lesson to rest. For me, it was like a revolving door—I just kept going around and around. I'd go for the same types of relationships with the same types of men who needed some kind of saving. Until one day when I realized the one who needed saving was me. That's when my trajectory began to change. It really is a simple realization that can cause an immense shift in your entire life. When I began to put my energy into myself, others stepped up to help, and suddenly I was surrounded with support and love in ways I hadn't ever thought possible for me. It took me choosing to nurture my spirit, my soul, my light wolf within and to thank the dark wolf for leading all these years, but it was time to rest awhile. There was a new sense of balance emerging, and it felt absolutely divine. It was in those moments of trust that I was able to expand on who I was becoming and dismantle who I thought I had to be.

It's a beautiful experience to come home to yourself. To feel the wholeness of your being as it wraps you in divine love. It took my entire world to fall apart in order for me to get put back together, and I didn't do it alone. I found incredible people within my community, and I created several tribes of women all rediscovering themselves as well. We looked to one another for encouragement, love, and support—I am forever grateful for all of them. I was also fortunate enough to connect with a wonderful and special man who became a trusted friend during my rebirth. He held me as I grieved, and he allowed me to heal at my own pace. Never forcing, never expecting, only ever supporting. My growth and healing process may have taken me many more years had it not been for his loving friendship and the incredible support system the universe helped me create. My relationships have evolved in the most incredible ways. The people I surround myself with today know the real me, the me that I built with intention and patience. My man allowed me the space I needed to discover who I am through aloneness. My friends witnessed me become the powerful and wild woman I am today and accept me without question. I feel incredible in my own skin, confident in myself and fully trusting of the divine timing of my life.

I'd like to offer you three guiding words that helped me along my journey of waking the wild within me. Trust, because you're going to have to put your faith into the Universe and all that is happening FOR you and not TO you. Compassion, because you will need it both for showering on to you as you put yourself under a microscope and taking radical responsibility. The final word is enchantment, because you have to believe in a power outside yourself, a magic-like whimsy that it's all going to work out as it's meant to. I know firsthand that it's not easy to remember our intuitive nature and to realize that we have endless knowledge from the universe within us, but allow yourself to swim in the possibilities and see what happens. Your life as you know it may evolve in mysterious and incredible ways. Believe that.

The Cherokee story I mentioned earlier ends with the grandfather telling his grandson that the wolf who wins is the one you feed. My own take on that story is that they both must be equally fed. The two are not at war with one another, they are in fact both fighting for the same thing—for our soul to discover its true power and purpose. They are polar opposites, which makes them the perfect pair to lead us through our lifetime. There are times when it is necessary for the dark wolf to bare its protective teeth, just as there are moments for the light wolf to allow you to embody peace among chaos. One is powerful and reckless while the other is compassionate and spiritual. Together, in unison, and in balance, one can embody this wild within with confidence and a beautiful ferocity. Ultimately, it's up to you to decide how you nurture the wild within you should you choose to recognize it.

You, reading this right now, you have an essence inside you unique to this world. It is filled with knowledge from the Universe and is always supporting you. The life of your dreams is within reach. The essence that runs through your veins has been passed down from ancestors of worlds before ours. You are divine, you are powerful. It is time for you to stand in it confidently. Everything is possible, *you* are possible. How will you feed the wolves within you? Which wolf is taking lead? Or are you standing in your power and leading them equally? The choice is yours.

Wake the wild within you.

~I'd like to thank my best friend and partner, Jesse Maslanko, for believing in me and supporting me as I grew into the woman I am today. I dedicate this chapter to my family, friends, and many supportive tribes who have given me unwavering words of wisdom and love throughout my journey; you are all very special to me!

Olivia Shwetz

Chapter 7

Goddess, Thy Name Is Destroyer

Angela Joy Eby

Angela Joy Eby is a personal and spiritual evolutionary, pushing the boundaries of prevailing perceptions in culture and religion. Currently, she is writing the screenplay adaptation of the book *So You Don't Want to Go to Church Anymore* by Wayne Jacobsen and Dave Coleman. With her BA in English Literature and Communications and her MA in Biblical Studies, Angela has written, performed in, and directed many church theater productions and short films. She also has written curriculum and spoken at several women's retreats and facilitated as moderator for her spouse forum for Young Presidents' Organization (YPO) as well as multiple book clubs. She serves on the advisory council for Evolving Enneagram, which focuses on contemplative communal practice. Presently, Angela is in the developmental stages of creating her own mentoring practice, turning her passion for coffee dates, learning, reading, writing, spirituality, personal growth, and travel into transformational conversations, which will include one-on-one mentoring and retreats.

Angela Joy Eby

@angela_joy_1

Angela Taylor Eby

"I am the goddess of chaos—
Out of me come new worlds.
Dance with me if you will,
Within the whirlwind of change.
Few worship me, fewer love me,
But everyone who's been
Fundamentally shifted
Has been blessed by me.
Such love I have for you—
I will break your bones
To make you whole."

I stumbled into this leg of my journey with a bone-deep numbness. After a gestation of years and born out of heartbreak and denial, I labored until my life became more than I could bear and culminated with a stillborn called Weariness.

Have you ever heard the parable of the Shit Eater? The Shit Eater was this lonely little fish whose only job was to ingest the community's toxic dump, keeping the aquarium tank clean. Then one day she lost her taste for shit and the tank quickly became fecund with fertilizer. She finally had the attention of the other fish, only to fall under their angry assault for her failure to consume their crap.

I had become the Shit Eater in my life. I acted like Lady Liberty: "Give me your tired, your poor, your huddled masses yearning to breathe free, the wretched refuse of your teeming shore."[1] Standing strong, offering hope of a better life to others, my own care and feelings went ignored, by myself and others. Growing up in an evangelical church, I learned early on it was my duty to serve and sacrifice for others and deny myself—anything that I could possibly want was selfish, sinful, and must be put to death.

When I looked at my desires though, all I really wanted was to be seen, known, and loved, and to see, know, and love others in return. This felt like the truth of the Gospel to me. But all my efforts, while keeping the world spinning for everyone else, yielded no fruit in my life. I became more invisible, less myself, and felt no love from those for whom I sacrificed. This created an escalation of loneliness, frustration, and anger within me. I tried to rationalize my feelings away. I had to have more faith in unfailing love! Once they felt safe and secure in my love, I hoped they would finally see me, love me.

My struggle continued until 2013 when I was diagnosed with extreme adrenal fatigue. Lethargic from all my "shit" intake, I went to an integrative doctor. After numerous tests, my doctor discovered that most of my energy hormones were at "sleep" levels all day long (all but one, glutamate, which was overly high and communicating to me, "Go, go, go!") Since I wasn't sleeping well, they never had time to rebuild to healthy levels. I was like a car in a closed garage, the engine on, the foot on the accelerator revving, sitting in park—running on fumes and dying of carbon monoxide.

My diagnosis led me to do some deep work. Exhausted but unable to sleep, I began to get up in the wee hours of the morning. I read books on psychology like the Enneagram (Russ Hudson), ancient wisdom like *The Four Agreements* (Don Miguel Ruiz), and religious mystics (Richard Rohr). Inspired by the works of Hafiz and Rumi, I began to write poetry. I realized I hadn't been allowing my emotions (energy in motion) to move. They were stuck inside me, coiling like a writhing mass of snakes in my gut telling me, "Stop! This is poisonous! Let us out!" With the burden of being the savior of the universe, I felt like I couldn't release that kind of death and disease into the world.

And so, my poetry began to illuminate for me the disconnects in my life. I came to understand that unconditional love included loving myself, *taking care of myself.* I turned to some new teachers who taught me about vulnerability and boundaries (Brené Brown) and codependency (Melodie Beatty). I started seeing my life coach, Julie Edge (insideedgecoach.com), who took me through "The Work" (Byron Katie and Martha Beck), which taught me to feel the truth in my body.

As I continued my interior work, my religious beliefs became more deeply challenged. Jean Shinoda Bolen exposed me to the concept of the Divine Feminine by fusing Jungian archetypal psychology with goddesses, and Sue Monk Kidd illuminated for me the repression of the sacred Feminine within the church. I also read Caroline Myss's work *Sacred Contracts,* which helped me identify the specific archetypes in my life. (Archetypes are identities or expressions of personality that manifest and explain behavior.) I easily identified the Savior/Rescuer archetype in me—my whole life revolved around saving all the ones around me! I felt like a "good person" because this was a part of my identity; this was socially acceptable behavior. However, I encountered another archetype that I feared—one that I had resisted my entire life. I felt like if I acknowledged it in my life, all the effort I had put into being the Savior, being the Shit Eater, would be wasted. This archetype was the Destroyer—and the few times I had unconsciously given into the power of this type, I felt uncontrollable rage.

I knew the Destroyer all too well because I grew up with it. You see, my father had the Destroyer in him as well. As an adult, I rationalized his behavior. He was a Vietnam vet and a product of the trauma of war and childhood hardship. But as a child, without the ability to reason it all away, I only felt a bone-deep terror around him when his Destroyer was unleashed, feeling like every day might be my last.

Fast-forward. I married a man who was the polar opposite. I experienced from him no rage but also no connection to any deep emotions. I went from feeling constantly attacked to feeling completely ignored. Every time I tried to express my hurt, I felt him pull even further away, so I stopped expressing my feelings. It wasn't worth it to share my emotions if it only resulted in greater distance. Then my daughter was born. Fraught with pent up frustration, fear, loneliness, and anger, and not ready to be a mother, I barely kept myself in check.

Until one night, my two-year-old had a meltdown. Overly tired, she didn't want to get in the car and collapsed into a puddle in the parking lot. Somehow the metaphorical key to my Destroyer's dungeon appeared in my hand and I let her out. I yanked my daughter off the ground, threw her into the back seat and began spanking her. I swung my arm around as hard as I could, overwhelmed with the combination of utter shame and complete exhilaration at the freedom of my unleashed rage. I didn't stop until I was worn out. Finally collecting myself, I put her in her car seat and drove home.

This moment in my life was an awful gift. I knew if I did not get help, I would repeat the patterns of my father and his father before him. While I had a deep faith in God, it no longer seemed enough; I needed psychological assistance to untangle the repressed mess inside. For years I worked with counselors and groups, processing my past and working on my marriage and parenting. I danced around my anger, venting it in safe places but never fully addressing it.

Fast-forward to my adrenal diagnosis. As I did even deeper interior work, I began to see that the Savior/Rescuer archetype had her own dark side. Rescuing others from their own pain and choices wasn't good for them or me. With this understanding, I began to question my treatment of the Destroyer archetype. Yes, my unchecked rage hurt my daughter. But was I overcompensating? I had bottled up my frustration, denied my own voice, and shoved away my own negative emotions, storing them in my body. If her job was to destroy, the Destroyer would one way or the other. Denied, all that anger was burning through my adrenals. Something had to give.

If I had to face this Destroyer archetype, I needed to know more. Enter the goddess. I discovered that almost every single Destroyer goddess was multifaceted: she was a warrior who battled evil, injustice, and forces who threatened peace; she represented passion and change, destroying what must die; and she was almost always Creator as well—the life giver and life taker.

In our culture, we do everything to avoid dis-ease. We desire to be comfortable, happy, wealthy, and healthy. We shun discomfort, gloss over sadness, and dodge poverty and death. But for all this avoidance, every day we still draw closer to our last day. Living by this old belief system was actually killing my body. Acknowledging that something had to change in order for me to find healing, I had to willingly go through the valley of the shadow of death. My body was telling me what was happening within—I had damaged my body by denying my heart. If I could no longer live in a world of compartmentalization, I needed to let the Destroyer cleave the flood gates and break open the shackles on my heart, allowing myself to feel it all—joy, pain, rejection, anger, love, and forgiveness.

And this truly became the crux of my dilemma, my dark night of the soul. Was I willing to acknowledge this other piece inside of me? I spent more time in meditation. In the silence, stillness, and solitude, I rested in my center, and I began to allow the emotions to flow through me without judgment. The dam began to break. It was here I truly began to understand the world is not divided into two ways of being—good and evil. My old belief system was founded on this premise. In that way of thinking, there is love and hate, light and dark, life and death. But in this expanded way of being, I could see that everything is imbued with light and shadow and light is not always what is needed. If life is a circle, then death is a part of the circle. Some things must end in order for new life to begin. This is the power and the light of the Destroyer—she prunes away what is no longer serving life.

Providentially, it all came to a head during Lent. As I meditated on the life of Jesus in his last days, I was drawn to the story of his agony in the Garden of Gethsemane. He wrestled with his own fear, questions, and desires. Yet, as he concluded his prayer, he said, "not my will, but thine be done."[2] As I pondered this in my heart, I realized that all my misery was of my own making; my will was resisting what was already true and real. I had fought at all costs to stay in the light, but my reality was shrouded in darkness. And that was okay.

I finally yielded to all that I am. In that moment I felt the profound peace of being in the perfect flow of my life. I was congruent. I was connected. I was able to release my Destroyer from bondage, embracing her, loving her, seeing her love in the darkness. I let go of my woundedness, my need to be justified, my fear that I would hurt those I love—I let go of saving them from their pain because I could see that my pain was leading me on the path of freedom.

And with all of this awakening, something shifted, and I knew it was time to leave my marriage. I was free to let go of a relationship that no longer served the greater good in either of our lives. And because I was at peace with destruction, I stepped away in love, not anger. For perhaps the first time in my marriage, I felt like my love for my husband was truly unconditional—no strings attached.

Since then, I still struggle with my ideas of the world being black and white. Old patterns die long and painful deaths sometimes. I have to remember that sometimes my Savior archetype is up to no good, trying to convince me that others' business is my business. And sometimes I want to resist the Destroyer archetype because she is, by nature, a creature of change and sometimes I just want to rest. I have to acknowledge that sometimes I want to annihilate something (or rescue someone) because the power and control would feel good. Other times, I get out my pruning shears and cut away something that was depleting my energy, or I offer help to someone who just needs a hand, and I know that both of these actions are loving.

I have come to recognize that these archetypes are a part of my ego; they are tools to be used by my true self and an aspect of my unique manifestation in the world. But they are not the boss of me. With my poetry, my teachers, and my contemplation, I practice finding my center. I am learning to allow each day to be whatever it may be. I am trying to accept whatever emotions arise, consciously trying not to push them away or latch onto them, but to listen to their truth and see if it is true for me. And I have to tell you, in doing this, I feel much more aligned with my beliefs, my experiences, and my choices. Heart, body, mind, and soul are no longer living in different compartments. In this way,

I feel at peace with the Destroyer goddess. She is in flow and at peace with the Universe, armed with the tools to respond to Life, through creation or destruction, come what may.

~I dedicate this to my closest teachers:
my children, for you called me to live for my highest good;
and to those I call family, who have served as my mirror,
showing me that my business is not theirs nor theirs mine but
that we are all a reflection of the incarnate divine.

Angela Joy Eby

Chapter 8

Fragments

Jessica De Castro

Jessica De Castro is a dynamic visionary and natural entrepreneur. Her passion for innovation and tenacious desire to reinvent drives her toward creating the legacy she dreams of. Despite the obstacles that have come before her, she is a resilient leader and advocate who inspires others to cultivate a life they'll love to live. She dreams of continuing to create spaces where people can embody the extraordinary intricacies that make them truly exceptional.

When Jessica graduated from a world renowned academy for makeup artistry, she launched into an extensive career in cosmetic business development. Just three months into her new profession, she was promoted to a leadership role where she embraced the opportunity to inspire others. Raptured by the ecstasy of providing value, she thrived in the cosmetic industry for over ten years. Although she has since moved on to explore the world of entrepreneurship, she continues to exercise her many gifts through her new ventures.

Jessica's vivacious and magnetic energy is the intentional outcome of all her life experiences. She understands that people have an imperative decision to make when faced with grief or trauma that will dictate the direction of their life and wishes to captivate others to act on this personal power through her written work. At the core of everything she dreams is her family, and her burning desire that these very lessons will empower her sisters and loved ones to believe in the remarkable individuality that they breathe into the world.

Jessica De Castro

_jessicadecastro

Jessica De Castro

"The emotions turbulently moved through her, igniting her veins with a rage so powerful it was blinding. Her heart went numb. Her mind went blank. Then in the very next critical moment a thought crept in so calming that it sang all the anguish away. I feel because I'm alive, and I'm alive to feel. Even at the depth of this emotional valley, beauty waits for me."

My eyes open to nothingness.
A suffocating darkness
that embodies every inch of space
around me.
I try to call out, but I have no voice.
Where am I?
Is this a dream?
Fear grasps at me, panic rising within.
I inhale the sharp smell of cigarette smoke.
I exhale, coughing violently.
The smell evokes a powerful emotion.
A repressed memory is looming—
Peeking out from its safe place.
Haunted by the surrounding emptiness,

I want to run from myself.
I look down to the realization that
there isn't even a ground
beneath me.
Am I just suspended here?
Without even sound to greet my ears?
Nothing exists here except me—
if I even exist.
Secrets suffocate me
as I float through my thoughts.
Such a busy mind in this nothingness.
Such an inevitable fate lined up for me.
Tears emerge as I fight the emotions,
Taking strangled breaths,
Until I wake up.

****

I see it like a broken mirror. Its pieces shattered across my life. As I move through, I pick up the fragments and put them together. It takes time, but I have a vision. I believe that if I see this through, I will see my reflection looking back at me one day. I will see myself looking back, complete. There have been a thousand times on this journey of self-discovery that I have thought I am alone in this. Why do I think so much? Why do I feel so much? I know so many people that don't ask why, don't care why. They are content with being kind of happy. Okay with being okay. Somewhere woven into my story, I decided that life wasn't for me. I have felt so much emptiness. So much sadness . . . a kind of sadness that doesn't fit the meaning of any word, in any dictionary.

I imagine it's more intense than all the feelings in the world. There has to be a meaning behind these extreme emotions I feel, something better beyond all the terrible things that happen. I just can't accept that "shit happens," and no, I won't just "deal with it." Undermining our existential experiences, the power behind our feelings, seems like an injustice. The second I picked up the fragment that allowed my biological mother's pain into my consciousness, I became addicted. An addiction to self-discovery that steered me clear from the addictions that had robbed me of her. This particular journey sees no end.

I was born to a beautiful mother with an ugly truth. Heroin and other narcotics controlled her life, making it impossible for her to be a mother to me. My maternal aunt Tia Paula, with the help of my grandparents, took care of me instead. I had supervised visitation with my dad for a few short years that I barely remember. All I recall is his long curly hair and that we'd meet at PJ's Pet Store in Yorkdale Mall. At some point he stopped seeing me, and I never really understood why. I felt maybe he didn't like me, or maybe he was just too sick like my mom. Luckily, there were a few people dedicated to making me feel loved. One of those people was Scott.

Scott was Tia's husband. To me, they were one hundred percent my real mom and dad. They did everything with me like you would with your own children. I never felt like we were playing pretend or as if I were a burden to them. Just love. Tia and I had a rock-solid relationship, but Scott and I also had a very special bond. There were things about me that only he seemed to understand. He spent hours hanging out with me like he actually found me interesting. One day a week we would watch the television show *Cops* together and order Pizza Hut. Those are some of my favorite memories.

When I started to understand that Scott had his own sickness, I was heartbroken. My mom wasn't the only one being held captive by her addictions. Alcoholism began to rake through his life, tearing everything apart. I remember coming home one day when he was strewn across the stairs. I was scared, thinking he might be dead. I didn't know it was possible to drink yourself unconscious. I pulled him, shook him, splashed him with water—nothing. Suddenly my incredible and fearless Scott wasn't looking so good, and Tia wasn't having it. She had years of dealing with my mom under her belt and couldn't deal with another addict. Before I knew it, they were getting a divorce and I was moving with Tia to my grandparents' house. I loved Scott and needed him in my life, regardless of the difficult time he was facing. The last thing I wanted was to leave him.

In reflection, there are so many ways in which this experience disrupted my perception of my life. This one stable portion had suddenly crumbled. I went from seeing Scott every day to once every few months, if I was lucky. My strong, absolutely brilliant father figure was no longer there. I was ten years old at the time and didn't know how to express the disruption of emotions I was feeling. So out came the rage. Rage over my mother, rage over my father, rage about Scott, rage at my family for not recognizing my pain. I was just so angry at the world. I poured into my books to escape the reality of my life. I cried over the pages. My heart ached for the people in the stories. This deflection gave me a release of emotions without having to face my own issues.

Within the year, Joe entered our lives. When I found out that Tia had a boyfriend, I was pretty distressed. What if this man didn't like me? Would she leave me and go be with him anyway? What if she liked him more than me? Would she not spend time with me anymore? Would she not love me anymore? I couldn't bear to lose another parent; she was all I had.

The day I met Joe I was wearing a full set of armor. If I was going down, it wasn't without a fight. I was fully loaded with sass and full-blown preteen drama. Tia decided that we would all go see a movie together. Fitting as I wouldn't have much opportunity to interrogate him. As we walked into the theater, I suddenly felt like I may throw up. My I-Got-This attitude took a sharp turn into the danger zone. I started to panic, feeling all the emotions lumping into my throat. I knew this feeling all too well, but this wasn't the time for a panic attack. As Tia looked for Joe, I stood in a corner, looking down at the ground, trying to focus on breathing. I wanted to disappear but there was nowhere to go. A sharp pain in my eyes jolted me into the awareness that I was staring down into a bright spotlight on the theater floor. Ouch! I looked up to see nothing but bright white spots dancing around in front of me. At that very moment, I heard Tia approaching me, introducing me to Joe. I was a deer caught in headlights! I rubbed my eyes, desperate to see the person in front of me. As the white spots got smaller, and the pain in my eyes went away, I found the kindest eyes I'd ever seen staring back at me. Eyes that looked into my soul. He was nothing like I imagined. The peacefulness of his aura washed over me, and I suddenly didn't feel so bad. I went through the entire evening keeping it cool, looking for reasons not to like him. It was pretty hard. He was nice through and through.

It took months for me to fully accept Joe into our family. I stayed guarded and skeptical, making sure he got the full screening. I couldn't believe that someone could be so good. He was extremely calm and level-headed. No matter how bad my attitude got, he handled it like a pro. He loved Tia in a way I'd never seen anyone love anybody. They were absolutely crazy about each other. At first, I loved him because he made her so happy. But then I loved him for a million other reasons. Within the first year, the three of us moved to a new city as a family.

I was starting high school that year and was filled with worries and anxiety. But of all the things I had to worry about, he was never one of them. He was a great listener, he problem-solved with reason, and he played a critical role in that pivotal point in my life. He loved me like a father would love their child, so I found another father in him.

When I was eighteen, I had a dream that I was walking down the street and I saw my biological father passing by. He didn't recognize me, and I didn't stop him. I had never dreamed of him until that night. The very next day, I got a message on Facebook. It was him! He wanted to meet me and reconnect. Riddled with curiosity, I obliged. It turned out he wasn't so bad. We actually got along remarkably well and began our own relationship that felt more like really good friends. Joe, however, was still my everyday dad, and Scott and I stayed very close. The relationships were uniquely their own.

The deeper you get into self-discovery, the clearer your problems get. This realization hit me hard. As the eyes of experience started to see through the smoke of my childhood, I released some pains and realized others. One answer meant twelve questions. Nonetheless, aside from all the challenges and heartaches, early adulthood was filled with wins. I grew quickly into leadership roles and allowed the experiences of my life to shape me into a resilient and determined young woman. I was proud of myself. To top it all off, my mom and Scott both recovered, my dad and I grew closer, my grandparents were kicking it, I was in a serious relationship with a man I loved, and Tia and Joe were happier than ever. Just for a moment.

The year 2016 started the best way. Vacation! On January 14, my boyfriend and I left on a trip to our first hot destination together. It was amazing. On the flight home I was on a total high. I felt better than ever and hopeful for the new year. Little did I know this was in fact the beginning of the worst year of my life. As I entered my front door, my grandmother's face told me that something terrible had happened. As the words escaped her lips, my mind raced. Joe had attempted suicide. On January 15, while I laid on the beach, he checked himself into a hotel, laid half-naked in a bathtub, and cut his wrists and throat open with an X-Acto knife. What in the hell am I hearing? Are we talking about the same person? I couldn't muster a reaction because it couldn't compute. I cry for literally everything, including every single *America's Got Talent* episode, and I couldn't cry in this moment. I didn't even feel sad. The only feeling that was coming through was complete and utter shock. Four blood transfusions and ten hours of surgery had saved his life. He was alive. Maybe I'm dreaming? What kind of sick dream is this? I wasn't dreaming.

The doctor said Joe wasn't suicidal. They believed he was suffering from insomnia and that the incident was an extreme episode of psychosis. But Joe was never the same. I never asked him how he was feeling . . . not really. I never asked him anything about it at all. I was afraid. I didn't want to upset him or make anything worse. So I stayed silent. Life went on. And then it didn't.

All that had come together had fallen apart. Everything I thought I knew about myself, I didn't know. Strength? Resilience? Intuition? Nowhere to be found. Reality smacking me in the face with a familiarity I shouldn't have known. Distress dressed me in vibrant robes of disaster for all to see. The broken girl who needed to hear that first voice. Feel that first touch, the only touch, free of judgment perhaps. The voice that reached out for my tiny developing heart and grasped it in protection. I begged for someone to tell me that my heart was still developing, that someone was still protecting me, that I was still a clean slate. On April

29, 2016, Tia came home to find Joe hanging lifeless in our garage. There was no saving him. I wasn't there, but I've spent so much time imagining what it would have been like. I can see her face in my mind. Running to him. Grabbing him. I can hear her scream and cry out for no one. I feel so angry that she had to be alone. I wished so many times I had been the one to find him, so she wouldn't have it etched in her mind, something that no amount of time can unburden. Our poor Joe. Why did this have to happen? People say everything happens for a reason, but there is no reason for this.

I slept with Tia every night for six months. I couldn't bear to let her sleep alone. I wanted to absorb all her pain. I was so consumed with her pain and helping her that I couldn't deal with my own. I worked more hours than I ever had in my life. Just to be busy, just to keep my mind away from what was happening around me. This trauma was different . . . there was no seeing it coming and there was no making sense of it. There was never going to be an answer. How do you live with that? How do you accept that there is no answer, and there will never be an answer, to losing someone you love? About seven months in, it hit me with full force. I was in a deep depression and I realized something about my life needed to change. How could I honor Joe with my life? How could I take everything he had gifted me and make something beautiful with it?

Time was my only friend. As the days passed, the vibrant color of my robes seemed to fade. I started to blend back into my life and began to find the fragments of myself along its path again. I'd pick them up, placing them in their very particular places of comfort. Of knowing. The thing about feeling so much is that you always risk letting in the wrong things. You risk your mind being infiltrated by pretty poisons, taunting words. It's how you come back from the wreckage of your soul, how much of yourself you can reclaim from the damage, that matters most.

What parts can you replace with better parts? What can you learn for next time?

Suddenly I was obsessed with knowing. Joe was a seeker of truth and answers. He wasn't okay with believing things "just because." So I found myself analyzing every part of my life. Who did I have in my inner circle? Did I like my job? Who makes the clothes I wear? What is in the food I eat? How can I positively impact my community through my everyday choices? My lifelong path to self-discovery took the best turn. The more I learned about the world around me, the more I learned about my place in it. Knowledge was healing me. Empowering choices were driving me. The very thing about self-discovery that once scared me, thrilled me. I felt powerful in my ability to take control of my everyday. The pain never left me, but I could breathe, I could love, I could dream again.

I have learned that all the tragedies of my life have played an integral role in creating the person I am today. Although I still have days when doubt takes ahold of me, I persevere. I get up the next day and know that there are so many beautiful things to see in this world. That life can be incredibly beautiful, more beautiful than all the ugly. When my mind is clear, I love myself. And every day on this journey of self-discovery my mind is clearer. I see myself more clearly. I see my life more clearly. I'm not alone in the darkness. There is something in the nothingness.

****

My eyes open to nothingness.
A suffocating darkness
that embodies every inch of space
around me.
I call out, and a soft voice calls back.

I've been here before.
It's just a dream.
I find consciousness, in my subconscious.
I inhale clean, crisp air.
I exhale light all around me.
Everywhere I look, beauty appears.
I see mountains in the distance,
I feel grass beneath my feet.
I capture the feeling of abundance
And I revel in it.
The most beautiful sunrise I have ever seen
has appeared in the grand space
above me.
Has the sky always been so surreal?
The soft voice returns to greet my ears.
It's my young self waiting for me—
So small in the expanse of her universe.
I have a secret to tell her:
Resilience is her superpower.
She will overcome every obstacle ahead of her.
She will manifest the most incredible things.
In gratitude I bask in this moment,
Listening to our synchronized breath,
Until I wake up.

****

~ This piece is in loving memory of Giuseppe (Joe) Petrone. All the times you listened to my stories mattered. This is one tiny fragment of the trillions of beautiful things that your life put into motion. You are eternal through the love that lives on in memory of you. Until we meet again.

Chapter 9

Rising from Depression, Falling into Trust

Liz Prax

Born Elizabeth Anne Ames in Northern England, Liz is the only child of gregarious, religious, extremely philanthropic parents who hoped for a large family and were blessed with just one daughter. Leaving this altruistic, multicultural, sometimes exhausting environment, she grooved, studied (a little), and air-popped away her twenties in the City of London, occasionally skipping the Big Smoke to sail the coastlines of Spain and Africa and the blue waters of the Atlantic. Now settled in southern Ontario, with grown kids, twenty-six years of marriage, and twenty years in a law office precipitously behind her, she is finally stepping into her soul path—her god-given gift for creation, through first music, then art, and now writing. Finding a new spiritual framework for her soul and a tribe of supportive soul sisters and brothers, she has transformed from a legal assistant chronically hooked on antidepressants and in constant physical pain, into a vessel of divine love—allowing the beauty of the Universe to pour through her into a parched earth. A late-bloomer at fifty-six, she proves we are never too old to unwrap our gifts and reinvent our future.

Liz Prax

"When we don't give ourselves space to process our emotional shit, then our shit will process us and attack us and those around us, usually the ones we love the most."

Depression.

It's a heavy word.

At least we are beginning to say it and look at it with a little less stigma and judgment.

You know, my aunt had a very "bad back" for much of her adult life. It wasn't until she was in her seventies that her family finally started calling it "depression." Of course it was depression all along, but that was not so socially acceptable in twentieth-century Scotland as a potentially debilitating state. So "bad back" it was.

Make no mistake, she was *debilitated.* So much so that (at the time) pioneering electroconvulsive therapy was administered and consequently memories were lost forever. She attempted suicide and misery ensued when the attempts failed. My aunt never recovered from her depression; she never found peace or lasting relief. She died at eighty-nine, having struggled through layers of physical and emotional pain for countless years.

I come from a tiny family. I have no siblings. I never knew my grandparents. My father's sister was my nearest next of kin besides my parents. So whenever a doctor asked about my family's health history, I drew a blank. The only thing I knew was that my aunt had a bad back. And sometimes my dad too.

In my early twenties, during a difficult period in my student life, I fell into a depressed state—a feeling of "severe despondency and dejection."[1] Given my complete lack of knowledge on the topic or of any resources to handle it, I barely had any idea even what to call it. It was outside my experience of life, and somehow taboo. Fortunately, I was self-aware enough to know that I couldn't carry on like this, and I went to find a student counselor and staved off a more prolonged attack by leaving my course of study and finding a job instead—i.e., I changed my circumstances in order to change my mood. That's a great way to tackle short-term depression, by the way, if you have the freedom. Change your environment, change your routine, and your mood will change too. However, a word of warning. As Confucius says, "Wherever you go, there you are."[2] Eventually, the new will become old, and if you haven't dealt with the deeper issues, the "depression" will return.

Throughout my twenties, constant change was my drug of choice against the gaping void of "severe despondency and dejection" that lingered in my peripheral vision. I changed jobs. A lot. I drifted off frequently, by train, plane, or tiny sailboat, with little to no advance planning. Jobs, apartments, boys, and friends faded in and out of focus like a constantly twisting kaleidoscope. At the age of twenty-eight, I ran away to Bermuda, a faraway dot in the ocean where absolutely no one knew me. I ran away from the familiar, the routine, the known things, the safe things. But I could not run away from myself. Thanks for the reminder, Confucius.

Fast-forwarding five years, I found myself living a life I barely recognized. I was a wife, a mother of two fascinating little people I didn't know how to raise, and a secretary in a law firm, with no clear memory of how I landed there. I felt sidelined into normalcy, my passions dulled, my dreams forgotten. Not that I had ever really articulated my dreams, I just knew that I had them. Marriage, motherhood, and the drive to survive took me over. Trying to keep my husband, my employer, and my kids happy left no room for my own self-expression or development. Nor did it keep anyone happy, least of all me. There was no room, in fact, for anything more than an hour of TV a night, a half bottle of wine (or was it a bottle?), and an exhausted collapse into bed.

Stress became part of my body. I also snagged a few unfortunate injuries (there was a lot of falling) from which I never took the time to heal. None of this is surprising in retrospect as I was so disconnected from myself, literally stumbling through life. Stress took the bait and morphed into chronic pain and depression. The insidious creature I had fled from resurfaced and crawled out of my own internal Black Lagoon, from the void of darkness, and took hold of me again.

I blamed my husband. I blamed his own unresolved emotional issues for his treatment of me and our kids, never once looking at my own. I have come to realize since that we came together for the wrong reasons, looking to fill an aching abyss in each of our emotional landscapes. My abyss was the yearning for a connection to masculine father energy, absent for most of my life to that point. My partner's abyss was full of guilt, shame, anger, and fear around losing his connection to nurturing mother energy, as he did when his own mother died and he was powerless to save her. Needless to say, trying to fill our abyss with another person's energy is a fool's journey.

We were too young, too disconnected from our ability to self-express our truths, shackled by outdated religious and societal expectations and sensitivities that prevented us from speaking to each other frankly and as equals. We had no framework within which to heal our separate emotional wounding, so we took it all out on each other.

Looking back with 20/20 vision, it is clear as day. We, as practicing humans, need to process our emotions so we don't spit them out over everyone around us. Taking care to notice, honor, and give our emotions space to flow, time to feel and time to heal has not been a priority in Western culture. It is not what most of us have been teaching our children. We are taught (and then continue to teach others) to squish down emotions, deal with them silently, suck them up, and put on a brave face, because big girls and especially big boys don't cry, right? But when we don't give ourselves space to process our emotional shit, then our shit will process us and attack us and those around us, usually the ones we love the most.

This is deep, messy, and inconvenient but essential work if we are to find peace with ourselves, with those around us, and with life in general. It doesn't matter how long the healing takes, it matters how deep it goes. Our tendency to be impatient with ourselves, to push push push ourselves to rush rush rush through so we can get to the other side and be free of the emotional injury is detrimental to our well-being and to the process of rebuilding our emotional health.

Physical healing has been treated the same way in the Western world. We get sick, we injure ourselves, and we are told to take this pill, have this surgery, push through the symptoms, and get ourselves able to function again as quickly as possible so we can get back to our stressful lives and do it all again. Our culture of needing ever more immediate results does not support true healing that really changes the way we do life. Treating the symptoms of stress is one approach but taking steps to defuse our response to stress and dismantle some of the stressful structures in our lives is like teaching ourselves to fish rather than just waiting for the fish to show up.

So what exactly is depression?

Here's the definition in Western terms: "A mental condition characterized by feelings of severe despondency and dejection, typically also with feelings of inadequacy and guilt, often accompanied by lack of energy and disturbance of appetite and sleep."[3]

And here's a definition in more holistic terms I have put together over a few years: "Persistently dwelling in low vibrational patterns, suppression of emotions, anger and frustration turned inward, causing self-destructive patterns to take hold."

Traditional approaches to treatment

1. Medication: Western medicine's go-to solution—a pill! Preferably lots of pills.

I am aware this may not be a popular take. However, I speak from a long and often bitter history with medication. Here is the gist.

Antidepressants literally sucked the passion out of me. In general, they attempt to control our emotional landscape without any influence on the patterns that hold it in place. They may take a "normal" spread of emotions that are "depressed"—meaning they are all vibrating a little lower than before—and then turn down the volume even more, while also preventing them from dropping below a certain level. They squish those emotions into a nice self-contained box with no surprises and no sudden peaks or troughs.

Later in my journey came antidepressant "boosters," supposedly meant to enhance the effects of the everyday SSRI or dopamine inhibitor, but really just an off label use of antipsychotics. One drug led me into a brief emotional death. One of the most ghastly periods of my life. Fortunately for me, I identified the culprit within a few weeks and nixed it. The drug—Risperdal. Give it a VERY wide berth. Another one to avoid? Abilify—well I had to ask after a few months, "abilify" for what exactly? To increase my capacity to feel acute anxiety as my norm? If so, the drug was one hundred percent successful.

"Emotional numbness" or "blunting" is a very real process. There is a wealth of evidence showing it as a side-effect of most antidepressant medications. However, the medical community does not appear to be tackling it yet as a serious concern or a reason to control prescription. Medical News Today's online newsletter published an article written November 17, 2017, in which Jennifer Huizen states: "Common medications that are known to cause emotional numbness include:

Antianxiety drugs (SSRIs): A 2014 study found that 60 percent of just over 1,800 adults who had taken antidepressants within the past 5 years had experienced emotional numbness.

Antidepressant medications: A 2015 study concluded that one of the predominant, long-term side effects of antidepressant use in young adults is emotional numbness."

In a June 19, 2017, article for MD Mag, the author Kenneth Bender had the following to say: "Guy Goodwin, DPhil-neurophysiology,

University of Oxford, Oxford, UK and colleagues acknowledge that many patients treated successfully with antidepressants report that they have less emotional pain than during their depressive episode.

"However, many treated patients also report that they suffer from a restriction in the range of emotions that they associate with normal living, such as the ability to cry or to feel enjoyment," they remarked. . . .

"The investigators found emotional blunting reported by 46 percent of treated depressed patients, with slightly more frequency in men (52 percent) than women (44 percent). Depressed patients with emotional blunting had significantly higher total blunting scores on OQESA [Oxford Questionnaire on the Emotional-Side Effects of Antidepressants] than controls. There was no statistically significant difference between antidepressants . . ."

The discouraging conclusion of the study was this: "The strong association with depression means we believe the description of the scale (OQESA) should be neutral in relation to the causes of emotional blunting which may be multiple," Goodwin and colleagues indicate. "Indeed, the scale remains a work in progress requiring more data collected under double blind conditions . . ."

It's a bit jargonized, but I think they basically just let antidepressants off the hook. For now.

There is a time and a place for medication. It can indeed be lifesaving, as it was for me. However, I made the mistake of allowing it to become a fixed safety net I could not or would not dismantle. For seventeen years. I was not truly healing, I was only masking the pain.

2. Counseling

The Western model of counseling has focused on positive thinking, boosting self-esteem, talk therapy, etc. These methods are successful only to the extent that suppressed emotions are honored and given space to reemerge, to be felt and expressed and allowed to flow and dissipate. Sometimes venting to a trained counselor can certainly help us feel validated and understood. However, the underlying causes of our shutdown may never be addressed in this way, and our triggers remain our triggers until we take steps to defuse them. Given the right circumstances, we are powerless to prevent ourselves being sucked back into a downward spiral of negativity and hopelessness.

The jury is still out for me on counseling. When practicing counselors are themselves "awake, aware, and alert" in an integrated, holistic way, then counseling coupled with somatic and other body therapy can indeed be a route to relief.

When healing really takes place

To sustain a solid rise from the lowest ebb of our life-force energy, when our vibrational patterns are circling the bowl, requires more than a boost from a charismatic counselor or a quick fix from a course of antidepressants.

It takes a shift in our deepest consciousness. It takes serious work and dedication. It takes a willingness to throw our conditioning, our own personal rulebook, out the metaphorical window. It takes opening our hearts and minds to question and challenge ALL our core beliefs and structures, built upon years of ancestral patterning and societal conditioning.

There are many paths toward spiritual awakening. All are valid if used with intent. During a session with a Reiki-trained counselor, he delivered to me the immortal line "Become a clear vessel." From our few sessions together, this was the one line I remember, and the most vital. He recognized the signs of awakening in me, and all he could say was "Hang on for the ride, and keep your intent on becoming a clear vessel." By that I understood him to mean, work on diligently removing the triggers that kept me pulled this way and that in the murky waters of life and thus unable to find balance or clarity.

I am incredibly lucky to have found, finally, my healing community, my soul family, and my sisters and brothers in arms. I have been able to dismantle the safety net of drugs and float instead in the arms of the Universe.

I am now two and a half years into a medication-free life. I shattered the cycle of pain and depression. I am emotionally resilient, I have found my voice, and I no longer need to be a victim of circumstances that appear to be beyond my control. I am learning to trust my intuition implicitly. I am my own hero, my own first responder. I do not need to be rescued. I am supported by something way more powerful than any fire truck or ambulance or knight in shining armor.

I have given myself permission to love myself and be myself without apology; to follow the inner guidance that comes through when the ego lets go of the reins; to be a musician, an artist, a writer, a poet, a dancer. However the beauty and love of the Universe wishes to be expressed, I will allow it to shine through me unobstructed by the mess of tangled emotions I once called home.

Final Thoughts

As I write, I sit in the difficult emotions that surface when I feel my adult children suffer, and I feel my own inner child and ancient mother suffer along with them. The helplessness, responsibility, and grief for what they, and I, are going through are almost overwhelming. Almost. The beauty of acceptance and trust allows me to let the emotional wave wash over me without fixating on where things are going and how it will all work out for them. I know they are on their own soul journeys, and that in some way they have chosen their experience. As I have chosen mine. We are inextricably linked, but we are also responsible for our own lives.

Emotions can be destructive or constructive. We get to choose our experience. We have CHOICE. We can allow feelings to consume us and suck us down into painful depths or up into heady heights. Or we can choose to alchemize them into a place of balance, peace, and acceptance. A place of equanimity.

Breathe deeply into your belly, the hara. Move your body. Put on your favorite dance music and bop around the kitchen. Do a little yin yoga. Walk in nature without a cell phone. Ride a bike downhill in the glory of nature. Swim, surf, ski, skate, whatever brings you joy. All will help to shift stuck feelings, allowing them to ebb and flow until balance returns.

I choose not to dwell in the dead zone of depression or the realm of past regrets. I choose peace, trust in the benevolence of the Universe, and connection to an endless supply of divine love.

Freedom IS possible. For me, for you, for us all, past, present, and future. I hold hope that my sweet aunt's soul finally finds the healing she was unable to find in this lifetime.

-Dedicated to my Aunt Doreen, November 1927 – October 2017

Liz Prax

Chapter 10

The Divinity within Us

Megan Harmony

Megan Harmony is a badass woman of God who has created the Soul Full Podcast and Lightwork Healing: Unleash Your Inner Light Facebook Group. She's on a mission to ignite the flame in every soul she gets to shake it up with. Her thirty-six years of experience overcoming adversity and healing the wounds left from these circumstances make her the perfect ear to lay your troubles on. Her no-BS approach mixed with her healing presence creates a safe container to heal and move forward. From a very young age Megan had healing hands; even the kids on the playground wanted her to hold their skinned knees. She is a soul-led warrior who will fight for your soul's right to be seen because she fully believes in the mantra "No Soul left behind." Megan is an Arcturian Reiki and Light Healing Master. Having trained and studied with mentors such as Gabby Bernstein, Russell Brand, Caroline Myss, Marlo Ellis, and Sarah Swain, she combines her in-depth knowledge of the intricacies of deep-dive soul work to allow you to rise from the ashes of whatever is plaguing you.

Megan wrote in *The Great Canadian Woman: She is Strong and Free* and *It's Ok to Not Be OK*, sharing parts of her story on how she rose and healed. She has been featured on podcasts such as *The Great Canadian Woman, Own Your Choices: Own Your Life* and *Everyday Inspiring Women.* She has spoken on numerous different stages, sharing her experience from being spiritually bankrupt, having a spiritual reckoning, and being dead in the emergency room to being lifted so high off the ground she often feels she is levitating. Her coin phrase "Let's go heal the world with love" is the landmark of what she represents and the healing she provides.

Megan Harmony

@meganharmonytlc

Megan Harmony

Group: Lightwork Healing: Unleash Your Inner Light

"We are intricately woven sparks of love—
it is only we who doubt or question that."

I'm about to share part of my story with you, but before I do that, we have to talk about the God word because it's going to come up throughout, and I don't want you to see it and turn to the next chapter. I believe that the word "God" is just that, a word, one that I use to express the Divine power and consciousness that is within myself and all humanity. It's in you too. Each individual has infinite power available to them AND each of us gets to decide for ourselves what we understand that power to be. To keep it simple, God is love. Unconditional Love. So when I refer to God, I am talking about a loving power that brings us all together. It is the power of the human heart to connect with each other on a soul level. So, if the word God brings up animosity within you, please think of it as your own perception of God or Source power, whatever that may be. I fully believe that each of us gets to define and label our source of strength as we are most comfortable with, and for me, I call that power God.

I have navigated through my life basing choices on my emotions and how I felt. I was always connected to the divine nature that exists in us all—the bright Divine Light. Right up until the point where both of those things (emotions and Light) scared me and I decided they had let me down. Therefore, I shut them up, off, and out of my life and started to live based entirely on logic.

As a young girl, I talked to God about all the things that were exciting in my world and would ask for help with the struggles. When challenges arose, and there were many (starting with having to take insulin injections at the age of five), I shared with God and asked for support to help me navigate this new experience. I told myself that everyone goes through things and that I was given this opportunity in order to grow and because I could handle it.

As I grew, more and more adversity came upon me. I was able to face it with grace and ease and a deep knowing that good would come of it—that God had even better plans coming. I shared love with everyone I met. Unconditional love for each individual, for exactly who they were, even if their current representation was deeply traumatized and flawed. I would love on them and take them as they were. This has always been my superpower: deep soul connections, creating a safe space, and providing healing. Intrinsically, I knew that everything is made up of light and love. All of us are equal in this journey—we are just in different positions on the path. I was alive and excited, but the world and its chatter were starting to get into my heart space. I started to do things that the small still voice within me suggested I avoid. I started to numb the expansive light within me. Eventually, I was consumed by the darkness. I had experienced numerous losses and traumas. With each one, I dimmed my light and numbed my emotions. While I knew deep within me that to continue on in this way was killing my soul, bit by bit, numbing by any means possible had become my comfort zone. Until one day when none of the numbing agents worked anymore. I was left to face myself and actually feel the heartaches that had come to pass. I decided to ask for help to slay my demons and learned to seek spiritual aid. I had a soul sickness, one that led to me acting completely out of alignment from who I wish to be. I had become so deeply disconnected from my true self that the only way to reach the light again was through spiritual practices. I prayed, meditated, reflected daily, and allowed myself to feel ALL my emotions. I can't be put into a box and encompass societal norms; that's not who I am. I sought counseling around the deep wounds of surviving a loved one's suicide, sexual assault, and domestic violence, to name a few, and I started to flourish and was filled with a deep sense of gratitude that I hadn't died. I picked up the spiritual kit of tools laid at my feet and my life became everything I had ever hoped it would be. I was given a chance to share with others the deep love Source energy has for them and how easy it is to access. Life was beautiful! I was an active participant in my life and God was my best friend, but I had some misconceptions.

I started to receive all things abundantly. My career became full time, which allowed financial affluence. The man I met and had fallen in love with received a job and moved so we could be together. My daughter trusted me. We bought my childhood home from my mother. It was as if I had arrived. I was feeling all the deep feel-good soul feelings. My friends started calling me "Spiritual Megs" and telling me I radiated God-light. I graciously accepted the compliment but didn't let it go to my head. Everything was truly magical.

Then came the days when all those material things that had been on loan to me from the Universe were no longer necessary in my life. One by one they dissipated. The only thing left was my relationship with my daughter, and I decided that I was not spiritual at all. These things were gone as punishment for the times that I had yelled at her, been insecure with my partner, or doubted God and my own inner light. My lack of spirituality must have led to this breakdown in my "happiness." I had lost myself in loving him, made him the priority in my life above my relationship with God and with myself, and when all those worldly things were gone, I broke. Not just a little, but a lot. Those endings left me with scars to remind me that the past is real. I knew right then and there that it was time to REALLY get to know Megan Harmony.

On one night my daughter was facing her own struggles, and I was trying to control everything in her environment to ensure her safety. My physical pain from my work injury was unbearable and limited my ability to do much of anything. I felt like I couldn't go on. I was reminded of an out-of-body experience I encountered in my early sobriety. I was six months sober and had had an emotional day. I was craving a drink but went to bed instead. I was drifting off to sleep and could see myself lying in the bed. It was as if I was in the corner of the room, almost as though I was watching a movie. Above my sleeping self there was darkness trying to consume my body and soul, while at the same time there was light protecting and covering my head and heart. Then all of a sudden, a flash of bright golden light encompassed the room with a loud thunderclap. My sleeping body was radiating bright light with a tiny sliver of dark within it. I had a deep inner knowing that I was in God and God was in me and everything would be okay. I slept the best I had in years that night. This experience popped into my head and again I knew

I AM OKAY.

I allowed myself to feel it all for as long as I needed to. There were many tears and pleading with/yelling at God, "Why did all this happen?" and "What the fuck was the point in all of this?" I went to the dark places of my soul and finally saw my light.

Awakenings can be painful
To become aware of the stickiness
To see the parts of you, you have been denying
To know deep within, you are meant for more
Makes you raw and exposed
Left with a decision
The only thing left is to expand
You could shrink and cover your eyes
Pretend you didn't see
The you, you want to be
But not you, girl
You open your eyes bigger
Step into your soul
And let your heart sing
BEcoming
BEautiful
BEing
BE

I rose up from the ashes of my last debacle and God saw me. I felt God and in that moment the world became anew. I saw people differently. I felt what they had felt. I became love. Whole, pure, infinite, unreserved love. And on that day she just opened up to all the parts she had been denying, all the parts she had believed were ugly, all the parts that she was fearful of. She opened up to the beauty in her whole soul. Not just the parts she had always enjoyed. In that moment of complete openness she was one with the divine where the light and dark combine. She was free to BE.

I had to let go of some lifelong conceptions that I had been holding onto surrounding spirituality and who I am. Being spiritual does not mean

I never yell at my kid
I don't ever judge people
I never cuss and swear like a trucker
I have my shit together every minute of every day
I am all these things and still spiritual and connected.

Nothing about being spiritual equals perfection. I thought it did and saw myself as not spiritual because I still did these things. BEing spiritual means being all these things without judging myself for them and applying spiritual tools if my shadow does show up as a reaction rather than a response backed by love.

My darkness showed up tonight in full force
It was me but is not of me
Temporarily it took the reins
And altered my mind and actions
I tried to fight it, tried to restrain
But she won out and her hellfire reigned
Followed by her judgment and self-hatred
For that which had happened
She tried to put out my light tonight
My soul the victor to retain
My physical self fell to knees and surrendered
Light bowed out to save the soul
And in so doing empowered all
Now dark and light combined

Are presented to you
Representing the Divine
The two live in me in perfect harmony
One step at a time
Holy Divinity Intertwined

I didn't believe it at all at first, but I started doing at least one loving act for myself each day. Not because it was part of the routine, not because it was on the to-do list, but because I made a conscious choice to love on myself each day. It was as if the voice of the Divine had said it to me and in that moment, I realized it had. I was a living and breathing piece of the Divine here on earth and all parts of me are made up of pure love. Here's the best part: We ALL are. We are intricately woven sparks of love—it is only we who doubt or question that. I sent gratitude to each person I saw. I gave thanks for each situation, whether it was a celebration or a trying time. I dove deep into prayer and meditation as an integral part of my day, and through that connection, miracles have continued to happen each and every day in my life. The most important relationship in my life today is the one I have with God (Divine power and consciousness). How I care for that relationship is by loving myself, all parts of me (light and shadow), because God is within us, in our soul space and never leaves us. If we experience something, God experiences it and feels it with us. That heartache, God cried with us; that health scare, God held us and was in it with us. It is we who turn away and try to leave the relationship out of frustration from not getting our way or fear of the divinity within us. The day I decided to stop running from my light and letting love in was the day that everything changed because I opened up to all the possibilities of who I could be and started living from my soul.

I remember that moment as if it were yesterday. I experienced a session with Cassie Jeans live and in person at an event that I had won tickets to. Yes, God placed me where I needed to be that weekend. At the end of the session when she asked if anyone wanted to share, with tears pouring down my face my hand flew up in the air. I was terrified; "Spiritual Megs" doesn't cry in front of a room full of women she doesn't know. This was full-on crocodile tears, and she certainly doesn't share her weakness. Obviously, with the tears I was called on, and I said something to the effect of "I NEED A TRIBE. I don't want to leave here and go back to my life and fall back into my old patterns. I want so desperately to have friends who are growing alongside me. I need you guys." Tears streamed down my face. I knew something had to change. I couldn't just let this be another empowering weekend that I enjoyed but went home from. My soul had been shaken. Many of those women are my friends today, and we have been through so much together—some incredible life-changing experiences as well as some heartbreaking pains. These women and many others are my soul supports now alongside my family, and there is so much love being spread around. You don't have to hide your frustration and imperfections, you need only find people who will hold space for you when your humanness comes out to play.

If I can leave you with one spiritual truth, it is this: You are amazing! You are incredible! You are the Divine in human form! Light beams off you even in your most flawed moments (in your mind's eyes.) Your imperfections (as you see them) are some of the favorite parts of your soul by God. Embrace all of you, every single cell, every molecule, because you are pure unconditional love. You have the power to heal the world through your incredible love, but first things first . . . it starts with loving yourself—the good, the bad, the ugly, ALL of your being, ALL of your essence. It starts with being kind to yourself and being gentle with yourself. With allowing yourself to screw up royally and being okay with that because it's going to happen. There's no doubt about that. Screw up on purpose and allow yourself to work through the torment you put on yourself in order to see that the world won't fall apart because you made a mistake. None of us are perfect spiritually, we are all just trying our best. So get out there and give yourself some love, 'cause, sister, you deserve it.

-For my daughter, Trinity, who shows me love in its purest form and encourages me to be myself. I love you, sweetheart. To every person who has believed in, encouraged, and supported me to see myself through your eyes, thank you. When I lost sight of the light within, you came and lit a spark to remind me. To God, my beloved, for loving me so passionately and never leaving me despite my doubts and fears—your grace has done more than I could possibly say enough thanks for. To you, the reader, for allowing me into your space and having the courage to believe in the possibilities that abound. Thank you.

Megan Harmony

Chapter 11

Awake the Wild

Khadoma Colomby

Khadoma Colomby is a lover of the deep. She is passionate about supporting women to live an authentic, wild, richly embodied, and pleasure-filled life. She is a mentor, guide, and leader for women to become intimate with and embrace the wildly feminine aspects of themselves. With a focus on returning home to the female body and soul, she guides women to reconnect with their deeper selves, supporting them in their exploration of living an authentic and intentional life by design. She teaches the power of simple rituals and offers guided meditations to reconnect with our feminine presence and power.

An aspect of her work is educating and empowering women in reconnecting with their womb wisdom, teaching menstrual cycle awareness, hormonal rhythms, and how to live with these cycles as a powerful sacred navigational system and gift in our lives. She believes this reconnection with the womb is an important aspect of the female revolution and a way to truly embrace all of who we are on a deep soul level as women.

Khadoma is also a songwriter and vocal coach and is passionate about using the voice as a tool for transformation and healing. Guiding with her sound and crystal bowls, she offers the journey of opening and embodiment through exploration of the authentic voice.

Being a self-declared multi-passionate woman, Khadoma shares her love for life in many ways, including 1:1 mentoring, hosting online group programs and sister circles, as well as educating and supporting women's holistic wellness in business and life. She teaches with authenticity and truth, using life as the path, and encourages presence to find the gifts within our challenges as well as triumphs.

Khadoma Colomby

www.khadomacolomby.com

@khadoma_colomby

Khadoma Colomby / Awake the Wild

Music recordings at: khadoma.bandcamp.com

"The female revolution starts within our bodies. In remembering the wisdom of our wombs and the deeper mystery of a wild and magical intelligence that lives within us."

When we really allow ourselves to be present, to connect with our bodies, our breath, our hearts, we feel. When we allow ourselves the wisdom of feeling, we experience a different depth of presence. We enter the unknown. The uncontrolled. We are raw, vulnerable, sensual, fierce, and tender. We cry. We break. We elate. We heal and crack open, again and again, to continue to *feel* ourselves *alive.*

Being a feeling woman is beautifully wild. This raw territory is held by the wisdom of the Wild Feminine. Instinctual. Embodied. Aching. Radiating life. She is an aspect of the true nature of who we are as women. She lives buried within each of us, in our naked truth and expression. She resides within our bodies and the deep wisdom of our flesh, our cycles, our blood, our emotions and intuitions.

We have been separated from our bodies and our emotions because they are powerful. We have been taught to doubt our knowing, hide our feelings, disconnect from what we know is our ground of being. Our wild, instinctual and raw self. Because it's powerful. It is time now we change this. We know it. Our souls call for a more meaningful connection to ourselves and our lives.

The Wild Feminine has been shamed and silenced for a long time. She is calling for us now. Speaking through our longings, our life questions and dreams. Calling for us to return to the holy ground of the feminine.

It is not easy. It's uncomfortable. It can be messy. And overwhelming. But there is no other way through but in. And there are tools to guide us through the dark.

****

> How do we feel in this world that teaches us to deny our feelings?
> How do we not become overwhelmed by feeling once we begin to open?
> How can we be strong and sensitive and find success in this masculine culture of the mind?

These are questions that I have pondered, lived and struggled with in my life.

The emerging feminine process is one that I am called to be a part of. The tears and fears shed, the real words, the vulnerability, the anger recognized and the release it provides. It shows me that I'm not alone. It gives me hope for our future. Through this awakening, we are reclaiming and recreating what it means to be a woman. We are rising together, holding each other and what is uniquely ours—our bodies, sovereign, untamed, fierce and feeling.

It is an incredible time to be a woman.

****

I have always been deeply sensitive. I *feel* my way through life. I am an explorer of the soul. I am emotionally raw and deep. I am creative and unfiltered. For as long as I can remember, I have felt like I did not "fit in." I tried, hiding my true self to be accepted and loved. But I always felt like I was too sensitive, too weird, too different. No matter how much I tried. Numbing myself with alcohol and drugs at an early age, engaging in sex too young to feel "loved," I always felt like an outsider, trying to fit myself into something that I wasn't, trying to be someone else.

You feel me?

In college the world opened up to me in a new way. In that expanding and disorienting time of the early twenties, I was exposed to the empowered archetypes of the Sacred Feminine. I felt a calling back to a world I somehow felt I had known. One that I had been secretly longing for. I dove deep into researching ancient goddess cultures, fascinated by an entirely different way of being in the world. One that was infused with art and ritual. Where communities lived with the rhythms of nature and the cycles of the moon, honoring the mystery and power of the feminine within life and death. I felt a stirring within me, as if some door had been opened. It was a way of life that my soul understood. It fueled my hunger for a different way of life.

This changed me. I found a missing piece of myself there. I felt known and comforted by something I didn't even know that I ached for. I went to women's circles, bonding with women who were deep like I was. *Here,* I began to feel a sense of belonging. I felt seen and valued for my feminine wisdom. I felt encouraged to tap into my intuition, empathy, and emotions. It felt like I had found a home. But, the bigger world around me was a structure that I still did not find myself in.

The world that I was expected to go out and make a living in did not provide me with a place to land. I could not see myself in the frameworks that were set out for me. It was scary and deeply isolating. Wanting to live a life of meaning, I felt outcasted, not able to find my vocation, my voice in the culture surrounding me. On a soul level, I felt like I did not belong.

And then, the fates led me to a small island, where I could live in the forest with the earth's embrace. I disappeared into the wild rather than trying to prove myself within a world where I knew I didn't belong. I honestly think that it saved my life. It allowed me to sink deeper into the woman within myself that I could not turn away from.

And still, as time and life progressed, and I felt the soul ache for more purpose in action, the inner conflict persisted.

What am I ***doing*** *here? How do I fit in? How do I serve?*

I was able to be myself within the safety of my community, but as I began to seek myself in a bigger purpose of service, I did not see where I belonged. I felt alone and invisible. I was afraid of sharing who I was. I hid myself in deep caverns. I shrank back my gifts in fear, unable to offer them out into the light. I experienced a deep descent of the soul and became depressed for a very long time. When we hide our true gifts, the unexpressed parts of ourselves become shadows and begin to consume us.

> Like Persephone, the Greek goddess of the underworld, I
> was taken down, into the depths of darkness and despair,
> to find my own light and declare myself as Queen.

Healing the wounds. Embracing my womb.

As I reflect on that time in my life, I understand why it was challenging for me. I am a strong *feminine* woman, and the world that I had been expected to fit into was/is extremely masculine.

I feel. Living in my senses, my intuition, presence and inner knowing. I honor BEING over DOING. I follow pleasure and inspiration. I prefer soaking in the moment over reaching for goals, booking my calendar and checking things off the list.

I was a voluptuous circle trying to fit into a square. And I did not "fit in."

So what was missing? What is missing for us now? And how do we create something new for ourselves as women?

Women's Wisdom was missing. The power of our wilderness embodied. The mystery and fluidity of presence and feminine power. The connection to and guidance system within our feeling.

This is an integral part of the intelligence we bring to the balance of this world. One that has been lost from the overconsumption of the rational mind. We have been trying to fit into a masculine structure and find ourselves there. But we, as women, need very different things than men. It is biological. It is in our brain chemistry, our hormones, our wiring. Not being supported in this way, we have lost an important connection to our inner compass.

To really know ourselves, *all* of ourselves in our dynamic feminine power, we need to consciously reconnect to our bodies, to settle into this fleshy matter and all the mystery it holds within its beautiful curves.

This task may not be easy, as we hold a lot of shame and wounding around the Wild Feminine. The years of trying to shape ourselves to fit into a man's world, stifling our feelings and fullness, numbing ourselves to create distance from our true emotions and the wonderful expanse we hold. Through our own self-sacrifice and hiding, many of us don't even know ourselves. This has created a lot of depression, hopelessness, and anxiety. I know I have not been alone in this.

It's time *we* create a new system in which we ***thrive.*** One that encourages Feminine Flow, feeling, senses, emotional intelligence, and intuition. A womb wisdom, based on natural cycles, cooperation, connection, co-creativity, authenticity, vulnerability, truth, heart, and meaning.

Womb Wisdom and Feminine Power

A *big* part of my healing into wholeness with my deep feminine came through tuning into my body's menstrual cycle rhythms as a path to female power. As I got to know myself more as a fierce feeler, I noticed that I experienced huge swings in my monthly cycle, from feeling like superwoman during ovulation to feeling like I wanted to disappear, curl up and cry during my pre-bleed week. This is a dynamic rhythm, one that was truly me, in all my phases. And it happened every month. Learning this information about myself, and how to care for myself in a way that was in tune with my womb, allowed me to be the truly wild feminine, feeling woman that I am. Through this, I welcomed myself home to my body, as a woman, and all the potency that I hold.

I knew that I had discovered something powerful. I gave myself *permission* to feel *everything* and learned how to care for myself in these varied emotional and mental states. I stopped trying to fight it. I stopped trying to hide it. I saw the value in my *cycle* and learned to value *all* of myself! The action and the rest, the outward expression and the deep internal quiet. The sensitive and the bold.

Through this, I felt a growing sense of self-love and belonging to something much greater. A connection to the wild dance of the cosmos, in all its cycles and rhythms. I was fascinated and began a journey that has brought me here. I researched female hormones, biology, and brain science. I talked to and interviewed women about their cycles and how they lived with them in their lives. I consciously aligned my life with my cycle rhythms and started empowering, educating, and coaching women to do the same.

Our cycles are our superpowers

Our monthly cycles are a very real and raw aspect of being in a female body. They are a monthly journey. Beautiful, uncomfortable, fiercely powerful and insightful. We are taken through the dark and the light parts of ourselves monthly. They connect us to nature, the seasons, phases of the moon, and our varied inner landscapes. We will experience between three hundred to five hundred menstrual cycles in our lifetime. And no one talks about this! Why isn't this a part of our education as women? And why aren't men also educated so they know how to best support us in these weekly shifts? Our menses is a shameful secret because it is a true aspect of our **superpower** as women.

I'm not just talking about the days we bleed, or the days before we bleed known as premenstrual syndrome (PMS) um, syndrome? As if there is something innately bad about this time of the month. I am talking about the whole month, of shifting hormones, neurotransmitters, moods, urges, energy levels, thoughts, and feelings. As cycling women, we are not static, maybe not even stable at times, because we are being constantly moved by the delicate dance of our hormonal flux. And that is one of the many *beautiful* things about being women.

When we allow ourselves to *truly feel* these rhythms—the pain, the anger, the insight, the stillness, the fire and sexual drive, creativity, and depth, we experience an incredible gift that is divinely feminine. We experience ourselves. Rather than hiding, numbing, distracting, trying in every way to be a straight line, we can embrace the curves of our dynamic beauty.

Aligning with your rhythm

Our cycles are a powerful navigational system. Each week of the month has precious gifts to offer us. Living in sync with our cycles is a powerful tool to rock with rhythm. It certainly has enhanced my life. I know and follow the flow of my own rhythm, taking care of the way that I feel.

I now rarely plan a date, social time, vacation, or biz launch around the time of my bleed, because that is the time my body calls me to rest, be quiet, go deep. That is the time for my Womb Cocoon. I want solitude and simplicity.

I know to make big strides in my biz and life, revel in my sexuality, and lavish in outward pleasures when I am ovulating, because that is the time I feel most radiant and am supported by my hormones and neurotransmitters to *shine.*

I am not forcing myself to try to feel anything else than what I am, and in that I have found forgiveness, belonging, self-love—home.

In Tune with My Womb

I know for many of us the idea of loving our cycles feels like a *huge* stretch.

But that is because we have been *taught* to despise our cycles. There is another way. It begins with a gentle inquiry into our bodies, our senses and their rhythms. A willingness to *feel* ourselves, rest there and value the wisdom of the deep. The reflective, intuitive, insightful, visionary, and still aspects of who we are.

This is a big part of our magic as women. A power that has been lost in a culture that overemphasizes work and accomplishment. It is in stillness that we find our wisdom, in the deep of our wombs.

So, how can we learn to embrace our cycles?

The first step is listening to ourselves, bringing awareness to our bodies and our rhythms, tuning into what brings us pleasure and when, how we feel when, *then* designing our lives, the best we can, around this wisdom. This intentional life-mapping allows us the space to *feel* all that we *do*. It is a way we can learn about ourselves and give ourselves permission to fully experience life—which is truly what brings us ALIVE.

"You were wild once, don't let them tame you."

~ Isadora Duncan[1]

So much of what it means to be a woman is to be fierce
feelers.
To see and feel, nurture and heal the life around us.
To bring our Sensitivity. Presence. Knowing and Wisdom.
This is a great gift within us. One to nurture and nourish.
To bring back the wholeness, presence and sensual nature
of being woman.

Reconnecting with our cycles is a pathway back to this. A journey of self-discovery. It is an empowering and vulnerable life practice to unfold into. It takes our curiosity and compassion. It has the potential to deliver us into our feminine nature and encourage the wilderness our souls are calling for.

It asks us to dive back into the emotional intelligence that lives in our bodies. The power to feel that is our wisdom. A gift this world needs us to return to for the future of our species.

We have a wilderness within our bodies that is still here, waiting for us to brave the deep and enter into the unknown.

Through a journey into the darkness of my womb, I have learned to love myself, all of myself, in my deeply feminine ways. I am here now as a teacher and guide, to support women to do the same, to encourage us all to feel and thrive in our beautiful authentic and wildly feminine selves.

I have found *home* in my body. I celebrate myself and my gifts through transmuting my shadows into the light.

Will you join me?

~ To all women, speaking aloud, seeking to uncover, braving the wilderness. To my mom, who always encouraged me to see the Wild in the world. To my husband, who has supported me in my deepest darkness and my blazing courage. To my son, who walks with an emotional intelligence that ushers in a new masculine. And to my little girl, who is a part of all that I do for women, building a future where she can walk freely in her wild and know she is loved.

Khadoma Colomby

Chapter 12

You Are Your Own Savior

Maggie Bowles

Maggie Bowles is the rebellious mystical poet and author behind the chapter "You Are Your Own Savior." She is a writer and brand ambassador for The Till, an online community dedicated to cultivating personal growth through positivity. Maggie is most passionate about helping others on their personal- and spiritual-development journies. She considers herself an Empath and Intuitive Guide. Her mission is to guide women into awakening and fearlessly embodying their truth.

Maggie is a life- and soul-purpose enthusiast. She believes we're all blessed with special and unique gifts that we are meant to share with this world. She also believes the only way we can keep what we have is by giving it away. Maggie has been studying mysticism and ancient teachings that promote these same ideas for over a decade. She became consciously connected with her spirituality at age nineteen when she first arrived at a detox center and participated in a 12-step program for her past dependencies to substances.

Maggie is most proud of her inner-soul work and being a single mother to her beautiful son, Eli. As of this year, Maggie will be celebrating six years clean and sober. She also struggled for decades with depression and anxiety and has now recovered. She spent the past six years working through thick layers of trauma, guilt, and shame that she had carried from her younger years. She now knows her past experiences can help others heal, and there is no secret to magically changing your life except for doing the inner-work and connecting to Source. Her promise to you is life will begin to open up when you start living in your truth, stop waiting for someone to come to save you, and become your own savior.

Maggie Bowles

www.maggiebowles.com

@maggiebowlesofficial

Maggie Bowles

"I love the way that in sharing our story, we can bring justice and healing to the experiences we've lived through."

We live in a world where, as women, our emotions are portrayed as our weakness. There's a worn-out school of thought going around, still murky in the air—the thought that our emotions, our intuition, and our monthly cycle are a misfortune. Intuition is thought of more of a hindrance than our superpower. Moreover, our emotions are just pitfalls that take over our mental capacity for fulfilling others' demands of us and work productivity. Our cyclical powerful nature has also had a bad rap from the beginning of time and is regarded as a curse. The world is unaware, in fact, that our feminine natural state and powerful emotions are our superpower.

Friction and unalignment arise within our inner and outer world when we are asleep to our true power. I once lived in the prison of the old belief system that my feminine makeup and my powerful deep emotions were my weakness. My wild feelings that no one could explain to me, that no one could help me navigate through, were a curse. Those primitive feelings were deemed my pitfalls. Consequently, this set a series of beliefs in my mind that I was incapable, unable, and disabled from society. If you can relate, I want you to know you are so perfectly put together and there is nothing wrong with you. You are here to feel your feelings, feel them without judgment and without fear. Feel them, understand them, transmute them, and work with your natural intuitive abilities to manifest the life of your deepest desires.

I long for every woman to know it is safe to feel your feelings. I long for this so deeply because it was not too long ago that I was still trapped in the mindset that I was completely and utterly defective and feared feeling my feelings. I had fears that if I fully expressed myself, I would make others feel uncomfortable. I still do sometimes fear taking up space and standing in my true power as a female, but I have found the tools and support to push through these barriers when they arise. The fear to express my true feelings sometimes still haunts me as well, but I believe in progress over perfection. All those years of fearing my feelings and intuition resulted in my complete separation from society at large and myself.

I felt like I was born into the world backward. Most people take a lifetime to acknowledge and feel life's interconnectedness to everything and your own Inner Divinity, yet I felt that connection to everything from the gate. My parents divorced when I was two, and there was a great deal of chaos in the separation. I created my own world to make things okay, as most children do. As a toddler, I can remember basking in the sun in a pretend cardboard box house, feeling the sun's warm rays on my skin with complete gratitude for his acknowledgment of me. I felt so deeply connected to the trees and the flowers and make-believe fairies; life was all so whimsical in my world.

As a little girl, I lived in my own world, and as I grew into a teenager, that did not change. When I was fourteen, I fell in love for the first time with my first boyfriend and my first everything. I felt this love so passionately, and when we broke up, I felt the pain so deeply. As a child and teenager with such strong emotions, emotions that most adults in my life at the time could not even feel yet describe, it was so confusing to me. This deep connection was a blessing and a hindrance for a child in this world. Looking back now I see that when I was a child, I began to fall under the veil of the fear illusion and began "separation" to self and others. I had no guidance to navigate through it all. I am not bitter or resentful toward my parents or teachers who could not counsel me through the repercussions of my highs and lows. I now have compassion and understanding that it was not their fault. I gain nothing by placing blame and empathetically understand now why people react the way they do when they're lost and in pain too.

I questioned the institution of school from a young age. It started with "Why do I have to be held back in class while all the other kids get to play on the computers?" I believed I was just a "creative speller and writer" and not at all delayed in English. Though the teachers were trying to be helpful, this consequence created more separation and reinforced the idea that there is punishment for being different. In my young teenage years I remember trying to figure out the riddle to the meaning of life. Life couldn't just be about going to school, making money, and acting like robots. I remember feeling this emptiness very deeply by age thirteen. I felt as if, if this was what life was about, I didn't want to be a part of it all. I felt like school was more of a prison, and I didn't understand why the teachers could tell me what to do. They told me when I could or couldn't go to the bathroom and what I had to learn to operate in this machine called life. School was difficult for me with the feeling of emptiness, and it seemed I was always getting in trouble for not knowing subject matter I had no interest in acquiring anyway. If learning all the answers was just to be a part of a world I didn't want to belong to anyway, I thought what was the point? I really didn't understand why I couldn't do what I loved more and make art all day and spend time outside. I had a lot of questions and a lot of feelings and a lot of confusion about our personal lack of freedom and choice. I definitely felt crazy and sounded crazy. I struggled to barely put my introspective thoughts about the world into words. I couldn't find the words to describe how I saw people asleep in a curated matrix among our systems and society. It was as if I were Alice in Wonderland, but the wonderland was a labyrinth of metal cold walls and I was trapped forever.

Teachers, my parents, my friends' parents, the police—everyone told me I was bad for being so lost and confused. I felt so lucky, though, to meet other bad kids who felt the same. We would do drugs, drink, and have sex to escape the nonsense and mundaneness of our robotic cold steel lives.

My emotions mixed with the cocktail of escapism turned on me. Pressure cooked me into a monster of anxiety and depression, self-hate and disgust for my very self. I was not worthy of love, I was a bad girl, I was a defect and unable to be a part of this world. I would leave the house for school, only to turn around as my body seized with anxiety, and the thoughts that I was an embarrassment, ugly, and fat held me back inside my home.

I spent a week in bed at age fifteen; there I was free from myself and the world around me. Cutting my own flesh began to feel good as I numbed out. My emotions were so skewed, misunderstood, and unbearable by this point. I learned that starvation could make me feel like I was floating up into the clouds away from everything here on earth. When I found my drug of choice at fifteen, I fell in love for the second time with the numbness of its powder potency. Twenty-six ounces of vodka was my drink of choice and blacking out was the only way I liked it. Consequently, I was suspended and then expelled at the lowest points of my high school career.

During this lost phase, my goals in life were not to become a doctor or a teacher but to be numb and hide and disappear from this hell I lived in. Not much changed in my young adult life, though I managed to graduate high school from an adult learning center and then went on to college. Shortly after postsecondary school, things got extremely dark, and it wasn't the first time in my life I lost my will to live. This time the devils in my head were louder than the feelings in my heart; I was out of control. I was stuck in a never-ending cycle of compulsion and impulsiveness, and I no longer ran the show.

I arrived in the rooms of 12-step programs at age nineteen, and by twenty-three, I had done two rounds of rehab and had experienced multiple stays in detox centers. Nothing seemed to tame the beast. At rehab and detox centers, I saw psychiatrists and tried pills; I saw ER doctors at all the hospitals, and no one could help me. I was searching in a bottomless pit of people, places, and things to save me from my misery. It all started to make sense in my young twenties when a doctor told me I have a disability called depression and anxiety. I was unable to work, and it would be better if I just focused on not using drugs and drinking. It was all such a relief, and I could finally surrender. I could give up trying to fit in, but it was also the label that completely crushed any confidence I had left in me. With my new diagnosis, I could now get the help I needed to learn how to "control" my emotions.

I was what they call "a chronic relapser" for half a decade, but at twenty-four I hit a new rock bottom. I had been in worse states of active addiction than at this age, but my spiritual rock bottom was different. It was then when I experienced my moment of clarity—it felt like a shining bright light for a split second in time. I surrendered; I really am an alcoholic-addict. The godly epiphany happened within the moments of wanting to end my life after drinking in a pub alone and attempting to self-harm once again. From there I mustered up the courage to take personal responsibility for my own healing. I became an advocate for my feelings and needs for the first time ever. It wasn't until I realized that no one could do the work for me that needed to be done that things began to change. I had to save myself and be my own savior, *then I began to heal.*

Luckily for me, my commitment to myself and healing journey took place at one of the most profound treatment centers on the planet. At this treatment center, facing my demons, I had panic attacks and hid under a toque and poncho in the group counseling. My growth felt like "one step forward, two steps back," but I began to be exposed to unconditional love by a surrogate family, the staff at the facility, and my heart began to slowly feel safe again in the world. An Elder at the facility taught me that "there are only two emotions in the world. Fear and Love. But only Love is real." I felt like I was finally accepted for the first time in my life for being me, being different, and feeling so deeply. This acceptance allowed me to explore my feelings safely and speak my mind without being judged as bad or wrong. I learned about universal energy and received energy healings. I was taught meditation and mindfulness. It was like the school of life and everything I had been missing to enjoy the gifts of this delicious human experience.

Things were peachy at the facility, and it was really just the beginning of my journey from my head to my heart. When the time came to transition back into "the real world," it was tough and lonely, but I held on for the ride. Since leaving, there have been ups, downs, deaths and rebirths. I now can say I once again feel connected to the stars, the moon, and all the beautiful people who reside on this earth. In times of darkness I can acknowledge this planet is completely out of balance and devastatingly twisted more often than not, though I know and believe change has to start with us as individuals. Our inner work must be done first in order to heal this planet. I've learned a lot of the time it isn't our responsibility as to why something happened to us, but it is always our responsibility to heal. In knowing that, I no longer need to dwell on the negativity and attempt to change things out of my control.

I long for all women who are still suffering from guilt and shame about their deep-rooted trauma and past to have the bravery to explore personal healing. I yearn for them not to run from themselves any longer and be done with fighting themselves for feeling. I pray for your restoration to feel connected to everything in this miraculous life. Embrace the power of your cyclical nature and the intuitive guiding force of your emotions. If there's one thing I can tell you from it all is to stop waiting for someone to come save you.

On my journey so far I've learned I am Love and I am here for a reason and so are you. Remember there are only two emotions, Fear and Love. Always aim to act from love. I believe anything is possible, and no matter how thick your conditioning, karma, or trauma is, we can always heal and restore to a life beyond our wildest dreams. I am living proof of that, and I believe you can be too.

~Dedicated to Charlford House Society for Women, Linda Shaw, and Linda Hazelton.

Maggie Bowles

Chapter 13

A Three Percent Chance

Erin Saari

Erin Saari is learning to live her best life. She is a daughter, a sister, a stepmother, a partner, an aunt, a niece, an athlete, a world traveler, and a survivor. Erin is a competitor at heart, always has been and always will be, and she's determined and adventurous. Some of these qualities may have led her to where she is today, living her life as a quadriplegic, but her persistence, perseverance, and tenacity have shown her that she is stronger than she could have ever imagined possible.

After surviving a near-death experience, her life changed drastically, but she wants to prove to herself and the world that it is possible to continue living an independent life once again. Traveling is a huge passion of hers and is something that allows her to feel free and truly alive.

Becoming an Olympic athlete was a dream for Erin as a child and now is a possibility once again—making the Paralympics is a huge goal that she will hopefully attain one day with the vigorous training on and off the track for the 100 meter wheelchair racing event.

Erin grew up in a small town in Ontario with a younger sister, Meghan, and brother, Kyle. Ann and Skip, their amazing parents, made their children and their love for sports their main priority, trying to attend every game and practice to cheer them on. She now resides in Halifax, Nova Scotia, with her partner (Chris), stepson (Nash), and her brother (Kyle).

Thank you to all my family and friends for all the support and encouragement. You know who you are.

Erin Saari

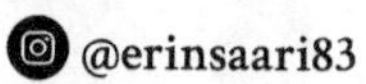 @erinsaari83

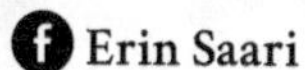 Erin Saari

"Life may never be the same for me, but without change there isn't any growth. I will make the most of this second chance and embrace the changes."

Persistence is key to creating your dream. Being optimistic is very important when trying to attain anything. I do not want anyone to feel sorry for me. I want the reader to realize how precious life is and how resilient the mind and body can be. We are much more than our physical being. Our body is a costume for our mind, heart, and soul.

It's important that I appreciate every small success, no matter what it is.

This is the steepest mountain I have ever attempted to climb, and this is merely a metaphor for the situation I am in. I have literally climbed mountains; I have scaled rock, climbing hands and feet, pushing upward toward the sun.

In my life now, post injury, with every few steps forward, it's inevitable that I will slip or fall down this treacherous slope, and it's unknown what will happen and how hard I will fall. Will I injure myself further? I must keep ascending. I will not give up.

Waving my head back and forth, eyes wide open, submerged in water. My eyes should be stinging—they are not. I cannot breathe. I'm yelling, swallowing water, bubbles are rising. I can see the water's edge like a horizon—I need to get there. Why can I not just stand? This pool is only four-and-a-half-feet deep. My legs will not move! Move! Stand! Kick! Listen to me, BODY—I control you. Please do what I need you to do; in no other moment have I needed your cooperation more.

My arms are floating, I can see my hand in my peripheral; why will you not move?! I am two inches from the air, from the oxygen I need to breathe—to live.

Someone will notice me. Help! Help! I can feel the heaviness of the chlorine-mixed water filling my lungs. I am so close . . .

I am going to fucking die.

Into the dark abyss. No pain. No further panic. Just soft, soothing—black.

Eyes wide again. I can breathe. There are those familiar faces! Chris! My love! Why are you wiggling my toes? Of course I can feel that. Move them? Move anything . . . no, nothing. I cannot move a single part of my body except for my neck, which someone I do not recognize is holding into place.

This has to be a dream.

Sirens.

Eyes open, tubes in my nose and mouth. White walls. Bright lights. I cannot move. I cannot talk. What is happening? Machines, beeping, alarms, unfamiliar noises. I cannot ask any questions.

Family and friends in sight.
I want to live.

"You have had a high level cervical spinal cord injury, and at this moment, after stabilizing your neck with rods and a cage, we are unable to tell you what your future holds. You have pneumonia. As of right now, you are on a ventilator and unable to breathe on your own. You cannot eat or drink anything as it will end up in your lungs. You have a three percent chance of getting movement back below your injury level, and you may have to depend on a ventilator for the rest of your life. There are no sure answers right now; we have to wait until the swelling dissipates, which can take up to six weeks, and even then, spinal cord injuries are very individual. What we tell you is based on the degree of damage to your spinal cord, what little movement you got back after surgery (slight bicep movement), and after some sensation testing we will be performing soon."

I am a quadriplegic.

I will never walk again? This can't be true. I can think my way out of this one, I have to. Just move, something—anything. How is it possible that only yesterday I was in the best shape of my adult life? I even took the classic bathroom mirror selfie that morning as an "after" picture to show myself how much leaner I had gotten in the past couple months because of my gym routine and extensive efforts to become the fastest woman on my tackle football team for next season.

Wait a second . . . walking is one thing, but what about scratching my nose right now? How can I do this? I somehow have to get the attention of the ICU nurse and then she will point to letters on an alphabet board to spell out what I am trying to say. By the time I finish it won't even be itchy anymore—mind over matter, I will think about something else—my life. Holy shit. This is my life.

A few meaningful diary entries after my injury:

Day 28

Last night after everyone left my hospital room, I lay in bed and began my nightly routine of sending messages to different muscles and decided to focus on my legs for a change. As I was trying to move my toe, telling it over and over to move, I saw the sheet move that was covering my body. I tried to move again, and I saw the sheet move again! I screamed and yelled for my neighbor to call the nurse as I couldn't properly press the buzzer with my cheek! My thigh moved! My leg moved!! I called my family, and my brother had just left moments before this happened and he came racing back! I have never been happier in my life. This is just the beginning!

Day 47

Today was amazing! I got to ride a bike! To feel my legs in motion, it's a feeling I have not felt in so long; the consistent flow of my legs pressing down was sheer joy.

Day 52

Today during physiotherapy I used a machine called the shuttle. The shuttle is a type of leg press, and I was able to press twenty-five pounds with both legs and press fifteen pounds with each leg individually. This was probably my favorite day so far.

Day 53

Today I was able to sit up on the side of the mat, feet on the ground, balanced all by myself, sitting there without anyone holding me up or the back of my chair pressed up against my back. It was all me! I could lean forward and back, stopping myself before I fell over; I call this a huge victory. Something like this may seem like nothing to everyone else, but to me, being able to sit up means that I may be able to stabilize myself enough to eventually stand and walk in the future. I know I will.

Life has been pretty good lately; not too many rough days at all. I have actually never had a rough day, but a rough hour here and there, and I'm able to overcome whatever it is that is bothering me in that moment and move forward again.

Day 65

> "Like minded, hard knuckled, always smiling . . . no-time-for-bullshit woman of awesomeness."

Day 150

> Don't worry tonight.
> Don't worry now.
> STOP.

After everything that has happened to my body, my mindset has forever been altered. I feel more beautiful, more aware or satisfied with every breath I take, knowing that I'm still here on this earth with the people I love and care about. When I see my body changing, the small seemingly unnoticeable changes that only show overtime, I recognize the resilience. When I see those muscles flexing and my biceps reappearing, my internal strength is showing externally. My tears of sadness have turned to tears of joy, and happiness, and strength. The love for my true "self" is new.

I feel much more beautiful now than I have ever felt in my entire life. I know who cares about me. I know who loves me. Most of all, I love myself inside *and* out. I had never truly felt outwardly beautiful until everything crumbled. My body was useless. All I had was my mind—thankfully, that was intact. I don't care that my nose is a little bit crooked now, or that my belly is not as strong and protrudes slightly, because this is me. Everything that I am now is because I have persevered. Because I've been persistent. Because of my resilient body and mind. I have been determined this entire time instead of lying around and feeling sorry for myself, which at times is okay. I've picked myself up, or others have literally picked me up. I've had to push beyond the limitations the doctors gave me and jump over that line that was drawn in the sand and see how far I am going to get.

To be told you will never walk again, and potentially never breathe on your own, is a hard pill to swallow. To believe everything you are told can be absolutely life-threatening.

I heard what the doctors told me, but I did not listen. I would not be told "my truth." I was going to live my truth and trust my intuition. I knew there was going to be more to my story; I could feel it deep within. With help from therapists, I learned to stop resisting my emotions, and I reconnected with my inner yogi. Meditation and grounding were part of my new daily routine. I was still not moving anything except for a slight bend in my elbows that was far from functional at this time, and I was more motivated than I had ever been in my life; family and friends helped to make this possible. I'm quite certain that the faces of my loved ones were what kicked me into survival mode, and I have always been a determined and competitive woman—only this time it wasn't a soccer game that I was playing, and the competition wasn't a neighboring city. I was up against the statistics, the percentages, the "will nots" and "can nots" . . . this was not how fast I could run or how many goals I scored.

This isn't a game at all.

Here I am today, breathing this oxygen that I was so sure I was never going to breathe again.

I am grateful for every moment I have now. I yell and cry. I still get angry. I get frustrated and feel sorry for myself, but I let it happen and I let the emotions take over. I've realized through all of this the greatest lesson, that I am not always strong. I need to stop thinking that I can control my emotions at all times; I need to let them flow, like a waterfall, or maybe a butterfly fluttering against the wind. Pushing these feelings away causes me to implode because they are not truly gone until I have felt them. No matter what, the unprocessed emotions are huddling up somewhere inside, waiting for the next time to try and show their faces, which isn't the right time because it is long gone now.

I feel. I am present. I am okay with looking weak because sometimes I feel that way. I know now that crying is the response to an emotion I am feeling; it is a release and it can mean many things. Tears can be happy, sad, frustrated, excited, orgasmic, and so much more.

I cannot grow if I do not allow myself to feel. Externally, my sensation is in complete disarray; the only "true" sensation is from my shoulders up. The new Erin, my new self, relies on memory of external sensation, so I want to feel all the emotions I can because I know they are real.

Becoming paralyzed is the scariest experience I have ever been through, and it not only affects me, but so many friends and family and even strangers. This injury has changed me physically and emotionally, and it has indirectly changed the way so many people that are a part of my life live their lives now. There is something to be said about tragedy and grief; there does not need to be a death in order to grieve. I lost a large part of myself through this event, but I believe that I have gained so much by going through the ups and downs. By properly working with the situation, no matter how terribly difficult it may be, the grieving process can lead to so much change and growth.

I would never say I don't miss my old life, or that I am positive every minute of every day, but I can officially and honestly say I love my life and the new experiences I have been through and new ones to come.

When I look back at everything I experienced before my injury, I am so grateful for so much of it. I made my dream of becoming a firefighter come true. I traveled the world and got to see and do so many things I could have only imagined. My life was filled with sports and activities, friends and family, and I wouldn't change it for the world. I lived in a resort town on a mountain for six years and snowboarded, hiked, and biked as much as my heart desired—and my body could endure. I'm glad that I took chances and created a wonderful life that I cannot only look back on and celebrate, but still continue to add to as my life goes on. There is no true telling what tomorrow will bring, so we have to make the most of today.

This is a new life for me; it is a second chance, and I have some of the same dreams and aspirations, and many new ones.

I am someone that my old self is proud to know.

~ This chapter is dedicated to my stepson, Nash. Thank you for making me the luckiest stepmom. You are growing up to be such an amazing, caring youg man, and I hope you will continue to follow your dreams and never give up.

Erin Saari

Chapter 14

Chasing Happy

Sabrina Greer

Sabrina Greer is the original *Boss Mama,* with two booming businesses built to support mission-driven mamas birth their brain babies. She is a four-time best-selling author, host of the five-star-rated podcast *You've Got This, Mama,* and creator of popular live events created for Boss Mamas. She "does it all" with three young boys, an eight-month-old puppy, and twelve egg-laying hens in tow. How? She has learned to curate the chaos and lean into the tough days and now teaches others how to do the same in one of her favorite roles as a Clarity Coach and Brain Baby Doula for women.

Her entrepreneurial journey began when she took maternity leave from her ten-year corporate career as an event planner and built a six-figure sales team for a network marketing company in less than one year. With a taste of what being the architect of her own life looked like, she never looked back to corporate, and never will. Sabrina wears her many hats with pure joy from her seventy-acre, rural "farmstead" in the woods. Sabrina is passionate about helping women, moms especially, discover their soul's purpose. When she's not workin' or mommin', you would definitely find her somewhere near the water with her favorite mama, Mama Nature.

Sabrina Greer

www.ygtmama.com

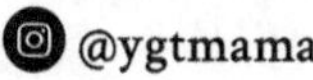
@ygtmama

ygtmama

"Our ego will not rest on this plateau, she must climb and persist for bigger, better, grander. Happy requires approval from others. Happy compares and criticizes. Happy is not sustainable."

I'll be happy when . . .

Have you ever muttered these words to yourself? "**I'll be happy when** . . . *I lose ten pounds. I make more money. He treats me better. My kids start school. I get that promotion. I finish that project. I have more time.*" Sound familiar? It's okay. I, too, am guilty of this incredibly human condition. Plugging "happy" into our internal GPS as a destination we will somehow arrive at "***when***" . . . Our brains have been programmed with this highly unproductive and in some cases destructive "*someday, one day*" mentality. We live in a society that feeds off instant gratification. We want a magic pill to make us thin and pretty. We want some secret code to embed in our hearts for the perfect relationships. We want the *get-rich-quick* opportunity to so badly not be a scheme. We are searching mindlessly for the secret sauce, buying into whatever false promises are tossed our way, believing the marketing, drinking the Kool-Aid, wondering why, after trying every single trick in the book, we still aren't happy. Not to be a party pooper, but if you are chasing happiness, this is likely the very roadblock stopping you from finding what you seek.

Let me explain . . .

I chased happiness for a long time, literally. I chased it all around the globe. I was what some may call a vagabond, a free spirit, a wander-luster, or simply a travel junkie. Labels aside, I was literally addicted to moving. With each trip came a new high, and then a low, forcing those searchlights back on. It was never enough, I was never content, let alone *happy*. That naughty inner voice yelling from deep within my psyche, wanting more. I consistently set unrealistic benchmarks and "goals" but never felt satisfied when I reached said goals. I suffered for a long time with what my therapists called "horrific anxiety" (this was long before the days of spectrums and socially accepted, generalized anxiety disorders), and I would tell myself: *This is normal! Success doesn't live inside your comfort zone, Sabrina.* ***It*** *only works if you do. Push. Force. GO!* Every failed relationship—*It's okay, Sabrina,* ***you'll be happy when*** *he gets through this phase in life, changes his behavior, does something different . . .* Every cruel judgment of my body—*It's okay, Sabrina,* ***you'll be happy when*** *you lose the extra weight, can fit into those jeans again, get new lips or a boob job . . .* Every drawn out, negative job experience—*It's okay, Sabrina,* ***you'll be happy when*** *you land that campaign, hit that sales target, get recognized for your efforts . . .* And every new country checked off the bucket list—*Hmmm, maybe* ***next time*** *it will be what you were looking for, Sabrina.*

You see, happiness is a response to an outcome. Let's let that one marinate for a moment. Happiness *demands* an outcome. The job. The number on the scale. The promotion. Happy is how you feel for a moment when you reach the benchmark, then it disappears, leaving an empty feeling in your heart. Maybe for a split second, watching funny cat videos on YouTube, you may *feel* happy. Your child gets a perfect score on a test, you do a happy dance. Your boss tells you that you are doing a great job, you pat yourself on the back. Sure, in these moments, ***happy*** shows up, but it's momentary, fleeting even. *Real happy* requires you to lose those ten pounds, right? *But then what?* You make more money, *now what?* Congratulations on your big promotion, *what's next?* You are flying to Germany in the morning, *yay! Okay, now where to? Happy* is not a realistic goal. Why? Happiness cannot be the destination because it's a moving target. Our ever-evolving definition of what this term means to us stops us from ever truly "arriving." Once we reach so-called *happy*, we want more, we crave MORE, we need more. Our ego will not rest on this plateau, she must climb and persist for bigger, better, grander. Happy requires approval from others. Happy compares and criticizes. Happy is not sustainable.

So who am I to be telling you all of this? You must be wondering, who is she, some kind of *happiness expert*? Not exactly; however, numerous sources define "expert" as *someone with comprehensive and extensive knowledge on a specific topic.* Doesn't knowledge come from a combination of personal experience and professional research? Okay, cool, then maybe I **am** a "happiness expert" as I've sure had my fair share of experience with this.

I want to dive a little deeper into my above-mentioned titles of "Vagabond" and "Wanderluster." My travel bug was more than just a desperate desire to check things off my bucket list and continue the ongoing search for happy. Years later and a boatload of self-work, I discovered it was an escape, a façade, an incredibly fun way to numb out.

I started traveling outside my home country, Canada, when I was only fifteen years old. Sounds crazy, I know, but I was one of those *as seen on TV* scenarios. Scouted by a modeling agency at the ripe age of thirteen years old, told I was more beautiful than the other girls, all-expense paid trips around the world, without my parents, attention from beautiful, exotic, older men, I mean, I really had it all, didn't I? So why wasn't I happy? I felt empty. The opposite of happy is unhappy, not depressed, which I was. I was depressed, anxious, addicted, and navigating some very turbulent waters for most of my teenage years. It was so much more than "angst" or "hormones," it was internal torture. But it made no sense at the time. I didn't grow up in a negative atmosphere. I didn't have a "tough upbringing." I was smart, good at school. I had everything anyone could ever want: a loving, supportive family, an extremely well-paying job (at fifteen years old) that involved monthly travel, a lingerie-model body, *what else is there?*

I know what you are thinking. If I am telling you happiness is not achievable, then what's the point? "If I can never be happy, then why am I here?" I told you I wasn't a party pooper—I am not telling you life as we know it is over and you will never feel good. What would happen, though, if we tweaked our thoughts and language ever so slightly? What if we stopped chasing happiness and began seeking joy?

"Isn't that the same thing?" you ask. Not in its energy. Joy is a state of being rather than a fleeting feeling. Joy is what turns up when we are living in alignment, doing what our souls crave most of all. Joy **is** the journey. It is the lessons in the difficult moments. It is soaking in the scenery flowing into our peripheral and allowing our GPS to recalculate without stress. It is surrendering to the greater plan. It is flowing peacefully downstream while watching the silly salmon struggle upstream. Joy is leaning into the discomfort that arises when the searchlights come on and learning how to adjust that light to shine on the deeper issues rather than the next quick fix.

When the novelty of excessive traveling wore off, I decided to turn to academics. I was twenty-four years old and was told "my modeling career was over because I was getting too old" and that "I should really start exploring other options for a career." I listened. I applied as a *mature* student (another blow to my shattered, old lady ego), got accepted to the school of my choice, and started a double major in social work and developmental psychology. *You may by now see a trend with my go-big-or-go-home attitude?* It was here I dove into studying the constructs of the human mind and was able to come up with a new diagnosis for my "depressed and anxious" self. I was, plain and simple, a *happy-chaser. Okay, this is not the textbook term and I totally made it up, but that, that right there had been my block all along.* I was always one step ahead of where I actually was. Translation: I was always wondering what was next for me. I was always looking ahead and freaking out over things that hadn't happened yet. I was wishing my life away for some idyllic future.

I once had a mentor share with me a gold nugget that I am now going to share with you. It changed my perspective, my view, my language, and by all means, my life. She said, "Anxiety derives from constantly worrying about the **future** and what hasn't happened yet. Depression surfaces when we dwell in the **past** or spend too much energy on what has already happened that we cannot change. There is no room for anxiety or depression in **the present**." Boom! Mic drop.

This explanation was me for nearly half of my adult life to date. Worrying about the future and what it would take to be happy and then dwelling on the past wondering what I could have done differently to have made me happier. No wonder I was a basket case. Are you still with me or have I taken you through a rendition of *Alice in Wonderland*

and down the rabbit hole? It may seem simple but when you are stuck deep in the toxic addiction of happy-chasing, it can be tough to get out.

So how did I do it? How did I overcome my "horrific anxiety"; how did I thank my depression for our time together before saying good-bye forever? How did I learn to find joy in literally every single crevasse of my world? How did I kick my addiction to happy-chasing to the curb? Obviously, I am going to tell you or I wouldn't be here writing this chapter for you.

I developed an ironclad system for finding joy and keeping it around. It all broke down to simple pillars, practices I could incorporate into my day with ease, small changes that made a big impact.

Pillar 1—Gratitude

This may sound like a trendy buzz word. Maybe you think you are grateful enough? Incorporating a gratitude *practice* into my *daily* routine changed the game for me. I emphasize "practice" because it is just that. You can't just say "I'm grateful" and call it a day. My favorite way to practice gratitude is to write down, every day, three things I am immensely grateful for, truly think about why, and thank said things. Practicing gratitude is a fabulous way to bring yourself to the present, and it is a great reminder that what we have is enough.

Pillar 2—Positivity

We have all heard some variation of the Cherokee story of the two wolves, right? We all have this internal battle happening between good and bad. Well, which one wins? "The one you feed." What are you feeding your mind to keep it from the dark? What are you feeding your soul to remind her that "happy" is not the goal, joy is? Fill your mind, body, and soul with positivity, good books (like this one), podcasts, music you love. We all have a choice of which wolf we feed.

Pillar 3—Abundance

This is a mindset shift. Having an abundance mindset means there is no room for lack. We have a deep understanding that there is enough to go around. Enough love, enough money, enough time, whatever your lack-block is. Living in abundance keeps you in your lane. There is no room for competition or comparison, just focus and alignment.

Pillar 4—Celebration

How often do you celebrate yourself? I don't mean those happy-chasing high fives and back pats, I mean true celebration for the little wins? *I kept a human alive today. I found space to breathe in silence today. Forbes* contributor Lelia Gowland speaks about the benefits of having a Ta-Da list rather than a To-Do list. This list is essentially compiled of all your small accomplishments; rather than seeing how far you still must go, look at how far you have come.

I still need to remind myself about these pillars, sometimes daily. More often than I'd like to admit, I slip into my old ways of *happy-chasing* now as a mom, a wife, a homeowner, and an adult human being. Every time my child pushes my buttons . . . *It's okay, Sabrina,* ***you'll be happy when*** *they are all in school full time, when summer camp starts, when you finally get to go on vacation.* Every time household bills pile up . . . *It's okay, Sabrina,* ***you'll be happy when*** *more money comes in, the house sells, when summer comes.*

Every negative judgment on the new version of my once-model body . . . *It's fine, Sabrina,* ***you'll be happy when*** *you have more time for exercise, can eat more than kids' leftovers, can take better care of yourself.* The difference is now, now I know what this is when it shows up. One of my favorite quotes is from author Gretchen Rubin: "The days are long, but the years are short."[1] This mantra is posted on my wall and always brings me back to center. The days do feel long sometimes, the minutes longer. Some days are excruciating to get through, but when we operate from a place of joy, we are reminded that the years are short and can find our way back to the present moment and relish in the beauty of every breath.

I am not a perfect person. I have bad days, days I wallow in self-doubt, days the darkness shadows my light, days I relapse, days I want to throw in the towel. Mainly though, I have days filled with true, cup-overflowing joy, but it takes work—painful, intense work. I can say with all my experience-filled heart though, it is worth it, you are worth it!

- To all the naysayers who never believed I could do the things I wished to do, thank you for the extra push I needed. To my husband, my rock, for showing me what true joy is; to my boys and my parents—for your unwavering love, guidance, and support.

Sabrina Greer

Chapter 15

This Is the Rhythm, This Is the Beat

Cassie Jeans

"Chills," "Goosebumps with every word," "I don't know what you did but I can still feel it weeks later." These are some of the phrases used when Cassie Jeans takes the stage, works with clients, or writes. When she speaks, her words are impactful and powerful, and she is known for being a leader that empowers the leaders. Her playful approach to life is warm and inviting, and her belief in humanity elevates everyone who comes into contact with her. She facilitates energetic healing and integrative mindset work. Her podcast is a valuable resource of inspiration and guidance, and she is active on Instagram, offering a range of inspiration and soulful words.

Cassie Jeans

www.cassiejeans.com

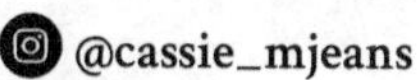
@cassie_mjeans

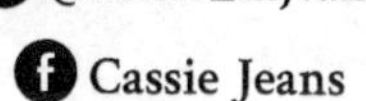
Cassie Jeans

"Our emotions speak up, allowing our intuition to guide us home."

And then this beat showed up,
I don't know where it came from
But I could feel it in every pulse of my life.
In the way I saw the world.
In the way I saw humanity.
In the way I saw myself.

A beautiful chaos of the worthiest kind.

I listened to this beat.
I listened to the way it moved me,
And oh how it moved me.

Some days I would be a puddle,
An absolute mess on the floor.
Then I would be exotic and captivating
Flourishing and alive.
Some days it felt like I could
Disappear and no one would know.
And then there were days of
A steadfast, steady call.

I loved the excitement of the rhythm I felt,
Even though at times the intensity
Knocked me off my feet
And yes, I crashed to the ground,
And the ground held me.

I loved when the rhythm let me dance,
When it didn't sway me into
Places I didn't want to go.
I loved when I knew the dance.

As I grew,
The beat grew
with me.
As I healed,
The rhythm
Made sense
To me.

Now, we dance together,
In the rain
And under the sun.
I know there
Is nothing to fear,
Nothing to run from.

And oh,
If feels so good to let loose and have fun.

Cassie Jeans

Moments. These vast moments before us. These pinnacle turning points, the pivots of our life. Often, these moments are attached to an emotion. *I was so tired, I just couldn't take it anymore. My life was a mess, I hated myself and everything, and I just wanted the pain to end. I tried to love him/her but living with the fear got to be too much. I don't recall what happened, but I know how I felt, and it was in that moment that I chose to be brave, and that's when everything changed.* And before we know it, our emotions have guided us toward or away from this beautiful gift that comes from within each and every one of us.

How did it come to be that our greatest power could be turned against us? How could generations of women be taught that being emotional was a curse? That having intuition was not real? That listening to one's inner voice was a mistake? That a woman's greatest weakness was that she was too emotional? Oh, the healing that has been done. Rest easy, dear sisters, our time truly has come. This healing is for all of us. Not just women, it is for each and every person on the planet and those who are yet to come. Breathe with intention and grace for all that we have learned and feel the joy of knowing our daughters will not carry this with them nor will our sons see us as the weaker sex. There is so much to celebrate.

There is also some real work to be done. Emotional intelligence and intuitive energy are some of the real joys of being a woman! Our ability to see beyond, to feel deeply, to be captivated, to fall in love, to know how to nurture our gifts. But too often we abandon this internal wisdom because of our own hunger, because our needs are not being met, because we don't know who we are. We create fights that do not exist. We create drama that is not real. We forget to listen to the wise woman within. We see our life, our body, our sex, our job, our marriage, our dreams, our art, our passions, and we compare them to others seeking the answers from a place of wound instead of power. We burden ourselves with shame and with guilt and we punish ourselves for choices we made when we did not know how to love ourselves. How can we expect our world to change if we chain ourselves to our past? How can we expect our sons and daughters to rise and live beautiful lives if we detest ours? How can we play the victim and let our hearts be betrayed and abandoned? We do this by listening to the voice within that craves peace.

Peace for everyone. Peace for this land. Peace for the chaos in our minds. Peace for the sanctuary of our souls. Peace for the frenzy and overwhelm. Peace for the past. Peace for the future. But most importantly, peace within.

Results are something I am learning to pay attention to. It isn't the easiest thing for me as a free-flowing, high-vibing, empathic, wild, passionate soul, but I am learning that results are quantifiable, and it is nice to be able to see data for the years of personal development I've invested into. Below is a list of results I'd love to share with you about what life looked like for me when I silenced my emotions and ignored my intuition.

- An inability to see how angry I was and a sense of entitlement to treat others based on how I was feeling at the time
- Empathic abilities on overdrive with no understanding of how to have boundaries and so I would save anyone that gave me any attention
- Scoliosis in my spine, X-rays that showed what anger was doing to my body from the inside
- Outbursts of rage toward my children
- Broken dishes
- Driving recklessly, wishing I could just drive into a pole
- Creating stories about people and shocked when they didn't fit into the preconceived idea I had about how they should be
- Thinking there was something wrong with me
- Inconsistency in my business
- Self-sabotage based on emotional whims
- Inability to step into my power
- Avoidance at any cost

I'm sure there are more. I'm sure some sound familiar. We are not required to tame the wildness of our heart, but we must learn how to use this power in a way that we are proud of. Not for exploitation, not for likes. We must do this lovingly and with reverence for the power of our emotions and the intuitive quality of our minds. What we feel matters. What we do with our emotions is our responsibility. Here is a list of the results of what it meant for me to claim my power:

- Inner peace—vast and expansive, delicious and available, transferable and impactful
- Inner freedom—the essence of joy circulating within my cells
- Inner knowing—trusting my voice, speaking my truth, staying open and flexible as I continue to grow
- Deeper, more meaningful relationships
- More satisfaction in life, less unease
- The ability to ground my energy with my breath
- Bigger impact
- Consistency and sustainable actions
- A love for myself that is nonnegotiable
- A belief in others that expands the Universe

And I'm sure here the list goes on as well. This has been a journey since infancy, and it continues on. In no way do we ever "cross the line" and arrive. We are in a constant state of ebb and flow. This is how we are designed for this time period. There is no need to try and answer all the questions that come up for us. More often than not we have to choose surrender and patience instead of giving in to the feeling that we have to know now and we have to be right about what we know. I agree to be a teacher and a student. This has allowed me to access momentum and to continue moving forward instead of being held back by my own wonderings. Breakthroughs are important, and in my line of work, I facilitate powerful breakthroughs for my clients. I know these are imperative for shifting energy and elevating mindset/soulset. But the breakthrough is like a climax. You know it's coming, and it offers a great release that is freeing and tantalizing—an absolute high. But there is a returning to grounding that takes place after a climax as there is a return to routine or habits after a breakthrough. The inner work focuses on daily shifts. The subtle ones. The ones our emotions guide us to.

You've read some incredible stories here. Real ones. From women just like you and me. "Horrific accounts of being human and the process of healing" is a title we could have called this book. We are learning so much about our energy and vibrations. We are learning the connection we have to our reality and how we feel. We are seeing people transform their lives, their health, their trauma through the process of meditation, prayer, energy work, sound, nature. We are seeing the effects of our negative thoughts and emotions and how they impact our world and our cells. The micro to the macro. The inner to the outer. The atom to the galaxy. All in one epic dance of life and our emotions are intrinsically connected to all of this and our intuition calls us to pay attention to it all. To remind us that this experience is a temporary one and the journey is what we are truly after. The only thing we take with us in the afterlife is our essence. How wonderful would it be to spend this lifetime curating our spirit? The soul is whole. The spirit communicates the messages from the soul. Let's make the decision to start tuning into that vibration.

Use your emotions as a way to develop awareness and resilience. We spend so much time and give so much energy to things that we could let go. This is a practice so use the stories in this book as a way to show you what is possible and lean on the wisdom of others. As you continue the practice of letting go you will find that you are held less and less by the things that bring you down. Picture it like a hot air balloon. Every time you release weight from your vessel you rise higher. Before you know it, you can peer over the edge and all the people and things that caused you worry, frustration, anger, resentment are out of view. You can only be held down by what you allow to be tied to you. If you knew you could access internal freedom and peace of mind if you started choosing your emotions, would you allow yourself to have this? It's available to every single one of us.

No matter what the experience, you can take your power back and you can let it expand so epically within you that you'll leave people in awe of who you are, but more importantly, you will be in awe of yourself. Why not take up space in whatever way that means for you. Each of us is being called to lead somewhere. When we are not distracted by our own emotions, our journey starts to unfold before us. One of the most powerful emotions for deep transformation is curiosity. The why beyond the reason. Emotional responses are habitual, which means that if given a different environment (your consciousness) we can begin the process of choosing how we allow emotions to guide us. Curiosity creates inner space for self-reflection. It's possible to overanalyze and self-reflect to the point of immobility and stagnation in your growth. Don't do that. Remember, we love peace and we love freedom. Become curious about why you feel the way you do about things, people, life, love, religion, politics, anything really. Do an energetic update. Do you still resonate with what you felt connected to twenty years ago? How about ten years ago? Last month? In the last five minutes? Probably not, right? You have changed. Are your emotional connections changing with you? Are you updating the emotional habits on a daily basis? This is the inner work that creates consistency with those breakthrough moments.

The women who have openly shared their stories with you are able to write about what has happened from a place of power instead of shame, guilt, reservation. Each of us is on our own journey, yet each time we share our truth, not only do we liberate ourselves we liberate others. How often did you peer into one of these chapters and feel seen? How many times did you breathe a sigh of relief because you recognized something within you had changed? This is the way we extend power and peace to one another.

We underestimate the impact that one person makes. We think we need to have an influence. We think we need a social campaign. We think if we aren't starting a revolution we aren't doing enough. We need to be louder, more demanding. Somehow, we have associated power with mayhem. Power begins in the silence. Power births from the brokenness. Power is when one woman states within her that "enough is enough. I am more than . . ." and claims her life back. The years after that statement are a frenzy of books, podcasts, gatherings, circles of connection, endings of relationships, beginnings of so much newness. It is our emotions that guide us to these places when we stop silencing them and give them space to be seen. It is our intuition that never leaves us and teaches us how to be responsible with the emotions, and eventually, we become a container of healing for others because we love ourselves enough to care about how we feel. As the healing continues, we have the opportunity to expand this healing even further and that is when we start to dance and play. That is when, rain or shine, we can let loose and have fun.

This is the rhythm, this is the beat. The eternal connection to our wild soul and the union of the spirit, heart, body, and mind.

An Affirmation to lighten the way.

I am safe to trust myself and the emotions that I feel.
I am safe to begin a journey that honors my existence.
I am safe to embody my truth and begin.
I am safe to feel even when the feelings are big and I don't know where to go.
I am stepping toward my freedom.
It is not a far step, it is very close.
I have walked here before.
Without restriction, without hesitation.
I feel peace now and it restores my life.
I feel peace now and it restores my life.
Here I am.
My soul has found me and it is very pleased.
I am,
All, within,
Me, and whole.

Repeat this as many times as you like.

- To the beautiful women who shared their stories in this book, thank you. To my publisher who created space so this book could come into the world. To each of you for reading this and feeling it. To my family who have held space for me and have mirrored my wounds so I could heal. I bless the journey and I am grateful to walk here now.

Cassie Jeans

End Notes

Preface

1. https://www.passiton.com/inspirational-quotes/7876-for-a-seed-to-achieve-its-greatest-expression, retrieved May 21, 2020

Chapter 1: Dr. Katy Spiewak, D.C.

1. https://www.brainyquote.com/quotes/wayne_dyer_384143, retrieved May 13, 2020

Chapter 4: Rose Finlay

1. Spinal cord injury patients face many serious health problems besides paralysis. https://www.sciencedaily.com/releases/2017/02/170216103931.htm, retrieved May 13, 2020

Chapter 6: Olivia Shwetz

1. The Story of Two Wolves. https://www.habitsforwellbeing.com/the-story-of-two-wolves/, retrieved May 13, 2020

Chapter 7: Angela Joy Eby

1. The New Colossus. https://www.poetryfoundation.org/poems/46550/the-new-colossus, retrieved May 13, 2020

2. Luke 22:42. https://www.biblehub.com/luke/22-42.htm, retrieved May 13, 2020

Chapter 9: Liz Prax

1. https://www.lexico.com/definition/depression, retrieved May 13, 2020

2. https://www.goodreads.com/quotes/3212-and-remember-no-matter-where-you-go-there-you-are, retrieved May 13, 2020

3. https://www.lexico.com/definition/depression, retrieved May 13, 2020

Chapter 11: Khadoma Colomby

1. https://www.brainyquote.com/quotes/isadora_duncan_145626, retrieved May 13, 2020

Chapter 14: Sabrina Greer

1. https://gretchenrubin.com/2014/03/the-days-are-long-but-the-years-are-short/, retrieved May 13, 2020

Helping Mamas Birth Their Brain Babies

At YGTMama Media Co., we help women bring their visions to life. Through a collaborative and supportive community, we truly value the idea that it takes a village as we bring your Brain Baby into this world. We are a unique and boutique publisher and professional branding company that caters to all stages of business around your book and personal brand as an author. We work with seasoned and emerging authors on solo and collaborative projects.

Our authors have a safe space to grow and diversify themselves within the genres of nonfiction, personal development, spiritual enlightenment, health and wellness, love and relationships, motherhood and business as well as children's books, journals, and personal and professional growth tools. We help motivated women realize dreams and ideas by breathing life into their powerful passions. We believe in women's empowerment, community over competition, and equal opportunity.

Join or Connect with The Mama Team

ygtmama.com

@ygtmama

@ygtmama